WOMAN

To: Mercedes,

There's a QUEEN
in YOU!

wear YOUR Crown!

Blessings

Praise for

WOMAN

"At a time when misogyny rules the charts and patriarchy rules the throne, Dr. Eddie Connor offers a beautiful paean to the extraordinary resilience and beauty of women. This unabashed embrace of the moral, spiritual and physical appeal of our women is a wonderful rebuke to the harsh and ill-informed assessments of women that pass for art or politics. Everyone who reads this book, will be blessed by its insights and warmed by its loving endorsement of the women in our lives."

- Dr. Michael Eric Dyson, MSNBC Contributor
Georgetown University Professor, Bestselling Author

"Through his book *WOMAN*, Dr. Eddie Connor describes the transition between the battle of brokenness into your breakthrough as a woman. What I love most about the book *WOMAN*, is the direct connection women can have through the vivid stories shared."

- Zakiyrah Ficklin, Author of *Her 20 SomeTHINGS*

"Dr. Connor's masterful and insightful body of work in *WOMAN*, will be helpful and inspiring to women, as well as men. The book facilitates in building a stronger awareness, of the (often concealed) challenges that women face today. He depicts the reality of both the joys and pains of life, in a very relatable and thoughtful writing style, by using corroborative references and levitating a silver lining through it all. *WOMAN* is a refreshing and uplifting read from a chivalrous, male perspective. One of his best works yet!"

- Dr. Jennifer R. Fuller, DDS

"If you thought *Dear Queen* was a sensational hit, then you are going to LOVE reading the book *WOMAN*. The acronym, *Wonderfully Orchestrating Magnanimous Achievements Naturally*, details the masterpiece of Dr. Eddie Connor's vault of knowledge. The book *WOMAN* represents empowerment, for the everyday woman. Each chapter empowers you to understand, how to attain your true femininity, identity, royalty, destiny, and extraordinary dreams. Dr. Connor helps us to break free from brokenness and bitterness, due to past wounds of unhappiness from unsuccessful relationships. After reading *WOMAN*, you will truly understand that your femininity, provides a remedy for the malady of life!"

- Dr. LaTonya S. Cross, DNP

"Within a stereotypical society, where women are forced to play by the rules, the alter ego of her existence is created. Her life becomes a contradiction to her inner self, which ultimately leads to those feelings of hopelessness and the inability to move beyond hurt. In this book, Dr. Eddie Connor outlines the epitome of a *WOMAN*. By the end of this book, readers will be blessed beyond measure, as it provides a blueprint for overcoming obstacles and becoming unapologetically whole."

- Ivy Nichole Neal, Founder of *Let's Have Girl Talk Mentoring*

"The book *WOMAN* by Dr. Eddie Connor, is a guide for greatness. It brings awareness to the plight and promise of everyday women, in pursuit of excellence. *WOMAN* reminds you to hold on to the gifts, that make you unique and let go of the defense mechanisms that keep you from letting love in. Regardless of how life has treated you, this book inspires you to stay connected to Christ."

- Dr. Ashelin R. Currie, Literacy Educator

ALSO BY DR. EDDIE CONNOR

Purposefully Prepared to Persevere

Collections of Reflections,
Volumes 1-3: Symphonies of Strength

E.CON the ICON: from Pop Culture to
President Barack Obama

Unwrap The Gift In You

Heal Your Heart

My Brother's Keeper

Dear Queen

WOMAN

Discover Beauty in Brokenness
and Wisdom from Your Wounds

DR. EDDIE CONNOR

norbrook
publishing

Also available as an eBook and Audiobook from Norbrook Publishing.

Library of Congress Cataloging-in-Publication Data is available upon
request.

ISBN 978-0-9970504-6-2
eBook ISBN 978-0-9970504-7-9

PRINTED IN THE UNITED STATES OF AMERICA

10 9 8 7 6 5 4 3 2 1

First Edition

To the greatest Queen and WOMAN
I've ever known...
My dear Mother, Dr. Janice Connor.

"Who can find a virtuous WOMAN?
For her price is far above rubies."
- Proverbs 31:10 -

CONTENTS

WOMAN

INTRODUCTION

I continue to ponder the question, "What really is a woman?" What is your definition? Give the question some real consideration and thought. Are you defined, by what you have or who you are? Is your value contingent upon, how much you have or don't have? Do you know who you are beyond your profession, relationship, or social status?

As a society, we are constantly inundated and oversaturated by images of what a woman can do, who she should be, and what she is supposed to look like. Oftentimes, these images are skewed, providing no real depth or value beyond the physical exterior. In the end, it leads to competition, chauvinism, comparison, and ultimately insecurity.

I think you would agree, that the true essence of

a woman is about more than what's on her. It's about what's

in her. As much as you admire your beauty in the mirror, it's

more than your smooth lips and sultry hips, that makes men

trip. It's not about your breast, legs, and thighs that will pop

eyes. Being a woman, is about more than how you wear your

hair. It's about more than what's on your head. It's about

what you have in your head. Beyond your physical assets, it's

about being an asset.

I'm sure you're thinking, what does a man have to say

about or to a woman? As a man, I can never profess to know

what it's like to be a woman and the vicissitudes of life that

you navigate. However, I must confess that you don't have to

be a woman, to empower a woman. Just like you don't have

to be a man, to speak to the king in me.

The word *Woman* is more than a noun, it's a verb. A

woman is action oriented. She doesn't wait for a hand out,

she extends her hand to help others up. She wears her crown and builds her queendom. She's royal and loyal, even sometimes to a fault. She's not chasing and waiting on a man, she works her God-given purpose and plan. A woman understands, that she is too unique to compete. She is her sister's keeper, so she doesn't have to compete when she can collaborate. She's not needy, she's needed.

My previous book, *Dear Queen* was a liberating love letter for leading ladies, to recognize and embrace the Queen inside of them. To hear and read the testimonials of women from around the world, who were empowered by the book, was rather awe inspiring.

Dear Queen was not some ethereal anomaly. It's a reality, about the value that resides in you. Many have asked me, "Where do you go from here and what will you write about next?" The idea is not to recreate the previous book, but to improve upon it. You improve upon it, by creating something new, fresh, and invigorating out of it. So with that

being said, I still have more to say. More life to impart,

wisdom to disseminate, and convey to our queens, our girls,

daughters, mothers, grandmothers, and to every woman.

I define the word *WOMAN* as **W**onderfully **O**rchestrating

Magnanimous **A**chievements **N**aturally.

You can't be a queen, if you don't know who you

are as a woman. If you don't have the proper mentality to

wear your crown, you will continue to drop it and eventually

lose it. The breakthrough and blessing, comes by building on

the blueprint. Any architect knows, there can be no house,

where there is no solid foundation. Essentially, you can't

walk in your royalty, without coming into the reality of who

you were created to be and your purpose for living. Your why

becomes the genesis, for what you can achieve and how you

can live your best life.

Finding your purpose is the key, that unlocks the door

to your joy and success. I'm reminded, there are two important dates in your life; the day you were born and the day you realize WHY you were born. What is your WHY for living? Beyond a marriage and a million dollars, foreign cars, fame, a spouse, multiple kids, and a house. Billions of people are existing on this planet, but very few ever really live. It's one thing to occupy space and breathe life, but to live you have to think and move on another level. Will you be the one, to maximize the moment and pursue your purpose?

The discovery of purpose, is the antidote to the ills of life. It's the balm that brings breakthrough. Undoubtedly, there will be challenges and setbacks. However, when you know your purpose, it only sets you up for a greater comeback. When you discover your WHY, you will find a WAY to bring the vision to fruition.

Purpose gives you vision and vision, puts you in the right position to win. Only when you know your purpose, can you see a bright day in a dark moment. Obstacles become the launching pads, that empower you to soar and shine in dark times.

At the age of fifteen, I was at my lowest point, receiving chemotherapy and radiation. Through it all, I had to trust God, believe against all odds, and adopt a mindset for victory. If we were watching *The Color Purple*, I would tell you like Sofia said, "All my life I had to fight." I fought to find the CAN in cancer, in order to be an overcomer.

My greatest opponent was not a hater, it was cancer and I beat both of them. Despite the battles and how broken life seems to be, don't lose hope. Don't give up. Keep believing and expecting, that things will work in your favor. Begin to dig deep and discover beauty, that derives from brokenness. I guarantee, your lessons will become blessings and your wounds will unveil wisdom.

Dear Queen was a beautiful paean, but *Woman*

empowers you through the ugly pain. This book symbolically contains eyes, to introspectively gaze into your life. It keenly peers into your dreams, your fears, your scars, your tears, and injects life into your life. *Woman* sees what you are, what you're trying to be, and what you're going to be. It unearths your value. It shines a light on your beauty, despite your past and mistakes. You're still God's leading lady. For all the hugs you didn't get, this book warmly embraces your true inner value.

As you read *Woman*, you will embrace your identity, femininity, beauty, destiny, and distinct royalty in a greater way. The quintessential qualities in you, are more valuable than anything that you could ever put on you. As you come into that realization, then reconciliation and restoration will begin to permeate your life. You're too great to be good, too amazing to be average, and too extraordinary to be ordinary.

Oftentimes, a woman like you is taken for granted.

You are a magnificent being, that only a divine infinite mind could conceive. Yes indeed, if God ever made anything better than a woman, He must have kept it for Himself. You are wonderfully made and divinely designed, with a purpose in mind. Even the beauty of creation resides within your womb, from conception to gestation. Beyond the radiant beauty that you exude, you are resilient and resourceful too. As men, we don't always appreciate you like we should. Yet you continue to encourage, inspire, and nurture the greatness within us, that we may not recognize within ourselves. The pain you go through, to look beautiful and smile, is not always easy.

Woman is a book, for the woman who has been through some trials and discovered strength in struggle. This book is not for the woman, whose life has been peaches and cream or never went through anything. If your life has been a bed of roses, then I want to address the thorns.

I applaud your steadfast mentality, even through

apathy and anxiety, to discover the beauty in brokenness. What you went through didn't define you, it only refines you. No, it doesn't make you worthless, just the more priceless. You are a beautiful woman, just the way you are. Each day your inner beauty glows, as you grow. You don't need to be a millionaire, supermodel, or "America's Next Top Model" to make a difference. You can be America's next top role model, by empowering and inspiring others to make a difference. You may never reach a million people. However, you may reach the person, who reaches millions.

I truly believe, that no nation can rise higher than its women. Continue to rise to the occasion, to speak truth to power and demand justice. Your impact supersedes an income. It's about creating an empowering outcome. You are the portal to power and prosperity. Don't minimize yourself, maximize your greatness within. You are smart enough, strong enough, powerful enough, and gifted enough to achieve the dream. Yes, you are enough! Don't doubt yourself or live in fear, because of the opinions of others or your own crippling ideals. Fear will paralyze you, but only faith will mobilize you. Get active and activate your unique purpose.

As you read *Woman*, begin to create a greater concept of yourself and your world. Use the wisdom from every page, to position yourself for promotion. Your next chapter, is greater than your last one. Despite hurt there is healing. The idea and dream that you let go of, pick it back up and try again. Remember it's not over until you win!

You're not a whiner, you're a winner. You're not a chump, you're a champion. You're not a worrier, you're a warrior. Rise higher, think bigger, believe greater, and work harder to manifest your destiny and dream. Even in my admiration of you, I admonish you to embrace the wisdom of your womanhood, the sensitivity that emanates from your femininity, and your nurturing nature.

Reach out and let me know, how this book has inspired you. I often say, "The revolution will not be televised, but it will be digitized."

Please connect with me, at **EddieConnor.com** for more information and inspiration. Friend and follow me via Facebook, Instagram, and Twitter: **@EddieConnorJr**. Take a photo with your book and post it on any of the social media sites, by using the hashtag *#WomanTheBook*. So, I'm ready and I hope you are too. Let's embark upon this literary journey, that will encourage and inspire you. Here's to you becoming a stronger, prosperous, resilient, successful, wiser, winning, and wealthier *WOMAN!*

CHAPTER 1

A Woman's Worth

*If you don't know who you are, someone will tell you what
you're not. For what it's worth, know your worth.*

T he Grammy Award winning and singing sensation,

Alicia Keys euphoniously, mellifluously, and melodiously

championed the worth of a woman. In her song "A Woman's

Worth," Alicia lyrically keys in on the fact, that "A real man

just can't deny a woman's worth."

Sadly, some grown boys have made the mistake, of

denying your worth. Realize their denial, doesn't diminish

your value. Rather it should expose you, to the greatness that

is contained within you. You can't expect others to see your

worth and authenticity, if they're blinded by their own

insecurity. Yes, I know it hurt because they rejected you, but it connected you to God and your value in a greater way. Find the blessing in the lesson. Someone who doesn't see your worth, is not worth your time. Remove the junk around you, so you can see the jewel within you. If you don't know who you are, someone will tell you what you're not. If you don't love yourself, someone will teach you how to hate yourself. If you don't see your worth, someone will discount it when you are priceless. For what it's worth, know your worth!

Your worth doesn't derive from what you drive. It's about what drives and motivates you. Your worth isn't dependent upon you having a companion. It's in you enjoying your own company. Your worth isn't contingent, upon you owning a pair of Jimmy Choo's. Rather, it's about how you choose to love yourself and others.

You don't need someone whose perfect, just someone

whose worth it. If they don't see your worth, they're not worth your time. The right one who is worth it, will be worthy of your time, love, energy, support, and serenity. They are worth it, because they know your worth.

HOW MUCH ARE YOU WORTH?

During many of my speeches, I often convey to the audience that the richest place on the planet is not Bill Gates' estate. Now that seems to be oxymoronic, when he as a business titan is worth $85 billion dollars. The "Queen of All Media" and visionary of the OWN network, Oprah Winfrey has $3 billion dollars. As a native of Detroit and loyal Lions fan, the Detroit Lions owner, Martha Ford has a net worth of $1.4 billion dollars. LeBron James, the self-proclaimed king who is seeking another championship ring, has a net worth of $400 million dollars.

Is it your house? If so, then sharing is caring, so please

give a brother a billion! However, the richest place on the

planet is neither of the aforementioned names, houses, or

estates. It's your local cemetery, because so many people

have died with gifts they never used, books they never wrote,

cures to diseases, and businesses they never started. The

tragedy is to be gifted, but never open the package and use

what is contained in it.

The issues of wealth and worth, are not only

interpersonal but also tangible. According to *The Insight

Center for Community Economic Development*, "Single

black and Hispanic women have a median wealth of $100

and $120 respectively. The median for single white women is

$41,500." The income gap is astounding. So how does one

determine net worth? Take all of your assets, subtract

everything that you owe, including your liabilities and the

result is a figure known as your net worth.

To analyze the gap further, single black and Hispanic

women have one penny of wealth, for every dollar of wealth owned by their male counterparts. They have a tiny fraction of a penny, for every dollar of wealth owned by white women. According to research, women of color who are divorced fare better, with a median wealth of $4,200. However, this is still only 26% of the wealth of divorced men of color, 8% of the wealth of divorced white women, and 5% of the wealth of divorced white men. As a result, many women cannot afford to take an unpaid sick day or to even have a major appliance repaired, without going into debt.

GENDER AND WEALTH GAP

We know there is a stark difference and income inequality, that creates the gender pay gap. According to a report released by the Senate Joint Economic Committee, "On average, a woman earns 77 cents for every dollar a man earns. A women's median annual earnings are $10,800 less than men's earnings." The *Institute for Women's Policy Research* estimates that the gender pay gap, will not be reached until 2059. What message does this send to our girls, young ladies, and women who do more but earn less?

As a whole, women earn 60% of bachelor's degrees, 58% of master's degrees, and 51% of doctoral degrees. Essentially, you're better educated than men, but paid less than men. Women of all races, experience a gender wealth gap, but the economic disparities are greatest for women of color. Sadly, women must work twice as hard, to only get half as much as men.

Despite the challenges, women of color courageously start businesses faster than any other group. However, as they go into business, many don't remain in it. Much of which, is due to lack of access to capital and mentors to provide sustainability. Wealth and wage disparities are interconnected. Lack of access to the wealth ladder and escalator, keeps people in the basement of bankruptcy and on the financial fringes.

What are the causes of the economic entrapment? Historical and racially driven policies, have often restricted women of color from asset building opportunities. As a result, it further exacerbates the wealth gap, rather than providing ladders of leverage for leadership.

STILL I RISE

Undoubtedly and unequivocally, women of color are the most resilient and resourceful people on the planet. Malcolm X declared, "The most disrespected, unprotected, and neglected person in America, is the black woman." Yet still, black women create something from nothing, start businesses, raise children, care for elders, create jobs, highly charitable, and share their time/talent to improve their communities. Women of color are leading ladies, in an ever-changing society.

Women of color are continually blessed, because more than anyone else, they can do more with less. Even with all of the statistics, that highlight the income inequality and financial frigidity. Women of color, still find a way to overcome anyway. According to *The National Council of Negro Women*, "Black women are more likely than black men, white women, and Hispanic women to purchase homes on their own." Against all odds, you're able to maintain poise like the poetic spirit of Maya Angelou who declared, "You may write me down in history, with your bitter, twisted lies. You may trod me in the very dirt, but still, like dust, I'll rise."

MONEY CAN'T BUY

You have something unique within, that money can't buy. A bank account can't hold it and your designer purse can't contain it. A resilience, forged by fire that causes you to rise in the face of adversity. The power within you, empowers you and others to transform adversity into opportunity. Through the heartbreak, bitter breakup, the divorce, losing friends and loved ones, financial woes, emotional turmoil, and trauma, you still keep pushing forward. You can't put a price on your patience and perseverance. Your ability to love despite hurt is priceless. Every tear you cried, released greater resilience in you. The price of your pain, is producing gain.

Many people gave up, they quit, and threw in the towel. Rather than give up, you made up your mind to get up and stay the course. This is the season that God is rewarding you, for your faithfulness and patience. Scripture declares, in James 1:3, 4 "Count it all joy, when ye fall into divers temptations. Knowing this, that the trying of your faith worketh patience. But let patience have her perfect work, that ye may be perfect and entire, wanting nothing."

See, when you change the way you look at things, the things you look at change. Realize this, what you went through was not punishment, but it was preparation for something (and maybe even someone) better. If you rely on God and remain patient through the process, things will work out perfectly. Everything will work together for your good.

YOUR WORTH MAKES YOU WORTHY

You have heard many times, that "Your network determines your net worth." Essentially, who you're connected to, determines what you're directed to. Realize that you can't get into the right places, by hanging with the wrong people. Watch the company you keep. The wrong network, will affect your net worth. Surround yourself with visionaries, go-getters, dreamers, big thinkers, and you will be influenced by influencers. Get away from people, who talk more about individuals, than they do about ideas. If they don't bring any value and worth to the table, then they are not worthy of your time.

Being worthy speaks to the attributes and intangibles, that you bring to the table. If someone asks, "How much are you worth?" Tell them "I'm priceless." You can't put a price on character, loyalty, honesty, good vibes, energy, real love, encouragement, support, optimism, and tranquility. These characteristics, should make someone worthy of being in your space. I'm a living witness, you can't put a price on peace. It's priceless!

LEECHES AND LURKERS

A lot of people have a hand out wanting a dime, but will only waste your time. They are not assets, just liabilities. They leech off you and lurk to see, what moves you're making. However, they lack the motivation to make any moves of their own. They want to benefit from your success, without putting in the sweat equity to get where you arrived. Guard your life against leeches and lurkers. These people will drain you of your energy, money, time, talent, and optimistic mentality. Beware. They will suck away and suffocate on your hard-earned success.

Get them out of your life! If you've hired them, fire them. Bless and release their mess, which produces stress. Forgive, move forward, and don't look back. Stop trying to go back and get the people, that God delivered you from. He put out the flame, so why rekindle a toxic relationship that was extinguished? It's a biohazard, to your benevolence and blessings. Let go and walk into the open doors. Surround yourself with people who are genuinely for you, not just for what you can do for them. They will enhance your worth, not diminish it. The people you can count on, won't discount you.

SEE WHAT I DON'T SEE

It's important to surround yourself with people, who have

vision. They can see in you, what you don't see in yourself. When you have vision, it produces provision. The right people who know your worth, won't see the worst in you, they will see and bring out the best in you. Simply because they want the best for you.

Their level of communicating, isn't crippling to your psyche and state of well-being. It's affirming of who you are and constructive when necessary. I've learned to never take "constructive criticism" from people, who have never constructed anything. What they deem to be constructive, is really destructive. Haters who see you rise, only want to shoot you down. They desire to tear your down, rather than build you up. See your value and know your worth. When you do, you'll attract people who recognize what you may or may not see in yourself. Stop stressing out trying to convince people who are not for you, to be with you and support you. It's not worth it, to force somebody to see you're worth it!

I GOT YOUR BACK

Many times in your life, you've been connected to people who say, "I got your back." In actuality, according to their actions, all they did was step back and stay back. Somebody who has your back, should empower you to move forward. They should put you in a state of progression, rather than regression. Having someone's back affirms, that you are their support system. They shouldn't strain your back, or use words that attack. Stop breaking your back and bending over backwards, to help somebody when it's hurting you. Stop breaking your back, to climb mountains for people, who wouldn't even jump over puddles for you. Surround yourself with people who bless you, not stress you. Don't seek revenge and try to get back at anybody. Just move forward by getting the wrong people, out of your space and off your back.

IT'S LEVELS TO THIS

If you don't know who you are, you will settle for less. When you settle for less, you generally get less than you deserve. As they say, "It's levels to this" and if you settle, you will never get to the next level. Remember it's not worth settling, just to say you have somebody. Save yourself the stress of jumping into a permanent connection, if you haven't healed from temporary pain. Take the time to love yourself, appreciate what someone took for granted, and know your worth in a greater way. You can't rise to a new level, if your mind is stuck in the basement. Deal with what's hindering you, from going to the next level. Living with animosity, bitterness, hurt, and pain will be a hinderance in your life, that constantly pulls you backward. You have to be free for your future and loosed, to go to the next level.

Develop a new self-concept that embraces your self-worth. Your mental health, spiritual well-being, and longevity of life are dependent on it. You have to expand

your mind beyond your block, boulevard, or background to

soar to new levels. As you think on a higher level, that is

where you will rise.

ASSET NOT DEFICIT

You are your greatest asset. No, I'm not talking about what's

on you. I'm referring to the value that's in you. In redefining

personal value, it must begin to extend beyond what you

drive, where you live, and what hangs in your closet. Your

voluptuous figure, financial and physical assets, don't

compare to you being an asset. Focus on what you're gaining

and becoming, not what you're losing. As you do personal

inventory in your life, you will begin to realize what you

considered an asset, was really a deficit. Begin to refine your

goals, values, morals, and standards. Retain what is an asset

and let go of liabilities, that are deficits. People that bring

division, will misalign your vision. As a result, they will

divide you from your destiny and subtract your substance.

What is intended to bless you, won't detract from you and

distract you. Pray for discernment to distinguish between,

what adds to you and what will ultimately subtract from your

value.

IT'S WORTH WORKING FOR

Like they say, "If it's worth having, it's worth working for to

attain it." Develop a mental picture, of what you desire to

achieve. Create a vision board. Write your goals. Connect

with an accountability partner, that will ensure you achieve

the standards that you have set for yourself. I don't have to

personally know you, to know that you have everything

within you that you need to achieve. When God created you,

He packaged you with purpose, promise, possibility, and

potential. This is your time, to deliver your dream and birth

your breakthrough. Don't look around, for what you already

have within. You don't need anybody to co-sign your dreams.

If God gave you the vision, then begin to run with it. Write your vision, read it, and run with it (Habakkuk 2:2).

Stay connected to the Source and you will have all of the resources that you need. As you seek God first, then everything else you need, will be added (Matthew 6:33). You can't expect to grow, where you don't plant. The harvest of abundance, is connect to the seeds of strength and substance that you plant. What you expect and intend on receiving, is worth working for to attain it.

THIS WOMAN'S WORK

The smooth soulful sounds, emanate from R&B singer Maxwell's falsetto, in the song, "This Woman's Work." Anyone with a pulse, can feel the emotion expressed from Maxwell's vocal gymnastics, that engender the song. He champions the struggle and strength, ups and downs, joys and pains that are idiosyncratic to a woman's work and worth. The process of becoming and being a wife, mother, business owner, caregiver, confidant, friend, developer, innovator, community organizer, and more under the title of "woman" is an arduous task in and of itself. Of all the hats you wear, you still manage to crown yourself as a queen.

Maxwell's voice echoes the words, "Give me your hand. I know you have a lot of strength left." Simply because, you don't know how strong you are, until being strong is your only option. As a woman, you have had to be strong in times of weakness. Yet God has renewed your strength, in troubling times. Through tests and trials, you realize that tough times don't last, only tough people do. For all that you've been through and what should have defeated you, God's grace empowers you to stand tall over and over again. First give God your heart and hand, so that He can prosper and multiply what is in it. As you give Him your hand, then He will give it to the right man who understands your purpose and plan. God has the right man, who will ask you for your hand. Yes, to put a ring on it. To care for you, lead, guide, provide, and protect you. The right man won't hurt you. He will add healing, to what God placed in your heart and hand. He will celebrate and value your work, thereby doing what it takes to make it work.

FAVOR FOR YOUR LABOR

Get ready! God is about to reward your labor with favor. All of your toil, the nights you cried, the times you were rejected, the naysayers, haters, critics, and the sweat equity rendered was not in vain. You are a blessing. You are a good woman that a good man, should be proud to put in the work for, in order to receive favor. Keep working while you're waiting. The right one will begin appreciating, the value that you bring to the table. As you sow the right seeds, your blessing will come to fruition. What you desire is worth working for, because you know your worth and you're worth it!

CHAPTER 2

Whoa Man!

A wise woman will amaze you and awaken the king in you.

Do you see yourself as God sees you? Do you have any idea, who you really are? God thinks more highly of you, than you could ever think of yourself. He sees you as a woman of valor, value, and virtue. Gospel great Marvin Sapp sang, "He saw the best in me, when everyone else around could only see the worst in me." You are the apple of God's eye. You are the crescendo of His creation. You are the zenith of God's zeal.

Realize as a woman, God didn't even put you on this planet until everything was in place. Understand that's how special you are. God doesn't bring you into chaos, but order.

If a man doesn't have his life in order and in place, much less his own place, then don't give him a place in your heart.

God didn't bring you into the earth realm, until everything was established. The trees, the seas, the land, the lakes, the rivers, waters, fish, foul of the air, the animals, and ultimately a man. After everything was in place, then it was time for a woman to come to fruition. You're that special, because you are the centerpiece of creation. You're not just the decorative bow on an expensive gift, you are a gift!

Once everything was in place, then God pulled you out of the man. God is not going to give you, to any random male. He wants to position you with the right man.

MALE VS. MAN

A male only operates in his gender, but a man walks orderly in his God-given gifts through respectability and responsibility. A male only defines himself, by what is below his waist. However, being a man is about what you possess, above the neck. Find out who influences the man in your life. Oftentimes, our brothers find it hard to express the love they are void of within. How can you be, what you didn't see? How can you be a man, if you didn't see or interact with a man? It's hard to play a role, if you weren't given a script. As a result, we operate out of frustration, because we were void of the proper representation in our lives. My dear sister, you've dealt with enough grown boys and immature males. As a result, all they did was break your heart. Wipe your eyes, don't worry but be happy. Something powerful is coming out of your pain.

BOAZ OR BOZO?

There is a real man with a plan coming, that's ordained by God to unlock your love and lift your life to the next level. Don't connect yourself to someone with no goals, no ambition, or sense of direction. How can you expect someone to lead you, if they don't know where they are going themselves? God will not release a man, if you are connected to a grown boy. He will not give you the right man, if you're still with the wrong male. He's not going to bless you with Boaz, if you're still dealing with a bozo. One of them will lead you into promise, the other into a pit.

ALONE BUT NOT LONELY

In Genesis 2:18, God said, "It is not good that the man should be alone; I will make him an help meet for him." If you've grown up in church like me, it's generally conveyed to us, that God is all we need. However God said, that "It's not good for man to be alone." Yet the prevailing question is, "How can I be alone, if God is there?" Consider and ponder that thought. If God is all I need and He is there, how can I be alone?

GOD IS NOT YOUR HUSBAND

Simply because our relationship with God is spiritual, but we are social beings. Breaking news, God is not your husband or your wife. I hear single women all the time say, "God is my husband" or "Jesus is my boyfriend." If you believe that God can keep you, then I'll agree with you. Praise His name if you consider Him to be the lover of your soul. However, if you believe that God is going to crawl in your bed and hold you at night, then I suggest you take your medicine.

Your relationship with God is not physical, but it is spiritual. Interestingly God said, "It is not good for man to be alone" while He is there. Simply because there are certain human needs, He will not meet. Rather, God will make provisions to meet your needs.

IS GOOD, GOOD ENOUGH?

God said, "It is not <u>good</u> for man to be alone." The emphasis on good, doesn't necessarily mean it's bad. The word "good" speaks to being beneficial, economical, or practical. It's not morally, physically, or financially bad to be by yourself. Yet the context of the text, speaks to the aspect that it's not conducive or desirable. It's not advantageous to the totality of happiness and well being, to be by yourself.

At the core of our human existence, no one truly desires to be by themselves. God created us to be spiritual and social beings. Although you connect to an invisible God, there are still times that you want to connect to someone who you can see visibly.

SINGLE AND SELECTIVE

The etymology of the word "alone" means to be solitary, separated, and isolated. It's interesting what God the Creator does. He says, "It's not good for man to be alone, after He created Adam by himself." Imagine Adam walking through the Garden of Eden, looking around and noticing two horses, two dogs, two elephants, two giraffes, two birds, and two lions together. Where is his partner? As brilliant as Adam was, I'm sure it didn't take him long to figure out, that he's the only one without someone.

God is above you and the animals are below you, but you need someone to be a suitable fit for you. Single and selective with standards, is better than lowering them for companionship with no compatibility. If you have somebody and they're not on your level, you're still alone! People often convey that God doesn't make mistakes, but did He overlook what Adam needed when He created him?

ISOLATION FOR REVELATION

Everyone that's married or in a relationship isn't happy. Every person who is single, isn't miserable either. If you're alone, don't allow the enemy to play mind games and make you feel inferior because you're isolated. In a situation of isolation, seek God's revelation for your spirit. Oftentimes, you can't hear God speak to you, when there's a whole bunch of people talking to you. Take the time to mute the noise around you, so God can speak to you.

Just because you're alone, doesn't mean you have to be lonely. You're single, because you're selective and you have standards. You're not single because you're ugly. It's because you don't want to be with someone, that treats you ugly. Yes, you can get anybody, but you need that special somebody.

Consider with me, that maybe you're not alone because you're inferior. Maybe you're alone, because you are unique and special. Maybe you're alone because you refuse to tolerate mess, when you have standards set for yourself. Refuse to lower your standards, just for the sake of having somebody. Getting anybody, doesn't mean you have somebody at all. It's better to be alone, than to deal with mess from messy people. I've learned that it's far better to be alone, than to be with someone who makes you feel alone.

MAKES ME WANNA HOLLER

We find that an omniscient God, was well able to deduce from the man He created, that Adam needed a help meet. So, God decided to make a suitable help meet for him. Genesis 2:21 declares, "And the Lord God caused a deep sleep to fall upon Adam, and he slept: and he took one of his ribs, and closed up the flesh instead thereof; And the rib, which the Lord God had taken from man, made he a woman, and brought her unto the man."

Allow me to put on my spiritual spectacles and Godly glasses, to conceptualize what might have transpired in the Garden of Eden. I can imagine God as a psychologist, probing into the man's mind. He anesthetizes Adam into a deep sleep. God becomes a nurse, admitting Adam to Eden Emergency Hospital. God then put on His surgical mask and gloves. He became a bone surgeon and cut the man open, removing his rib. God constructed the bone and created a woman from the man. God then became the woman's father, woke Adam up, and brought her to the man. God stepped back, became the preacher and said, "Who giveth this woman to be the bride of this man."

The man looked at the woman that God created and hollered, "Whoa man!" Genesis 2:23 declares, "And Adam said, This is now bone of my bones, and flesh of my flesh: she shall be called Woman, because she was taken out of Man." God gave Adam His presence, purpose, and a place, before he received a partner. God will create the perfect blessing for you, that makes you want to holler and throw up both of your hands!

SHE PRAYS AND SLAYS

To the brother who is reading this book, realize the importance of having the right woman. The right one will make you say "Whoa man" but the wrong one, will make you say "Oh man." The right woman will put you in such amazement and awe, that her standards will make you step up your game. She will upgrade your life and lift you to the next level.

As a woman, your lifestyle should make a man level up. In a world of quantity, being a woman of quality will make the right man holler "Whoa man!" He won't holler, because you're screaming and hollering at him. He will holler with excitement because he found you. The right man will thank the Lord for a woman like you, that He could only dream of receiving. Your aura and essence will make him say, "Where have you been all of my life?" You will make him holler, when he sees the magnanimous splendor of the beauty of your femininity, as you walk in your destiny. A woman like you that prays and slays in the boardroom, classroom, hospital room, courtroom, and any room you walk in, signifies that you're a blessing from God.

NOT BEHIND, BESIDE

I often hear the phrase, "Behind every great man is a great woman." I know it sounds good, but the phraseology is utterly wrong. It's not behind, but "Beside every great man is a great woman." I find it intriguing that God did not create the woman from the skull, so she could usurp his authority. God did not create the woman from the plantar bone of the foot, so the man could step on her. Neither did He create the woman from the vertebra of the man's back, so he could be in front of her.

Rather, God created the woman from the man's rib,

which is from the side of his anatomical structure. This is because a woman is intended to be, the right man's help meet and remain by his side. She's not just successful, but she's also helpful. Yes, even through tough times of tests and trials.

I tell women all the time, a man doesn't have to be in front of you, to lead you. He doesn't even have to make more money than you, to lead you. I just upset you now! You see a visionary man can lead you hand in hand, right by your side. A real man doesn't want his woman behind him. He wants her beside him.

ARE YOU DISMISSIVE OR SUBMISSIVE?

Like a rib protects the heart, a wife protects her husband. A husband also protects his wife, in the same manner. They submit to one another, as unto God. Are you dismissive or submissive though? The prefix "sub" means under. How can you expect someone to submit to you, if you're negative, nasty, and a nag? Do you have an understanding of one another, to submit to one another? Essentially, are you a headache or a helpmate?

Ephesians 5:21 declares, "Submitting yourselves one to another in the fear of God." The suffix "ing" means to submit continually, by doing it over and over again. Ephesians 5:22, 23, and 25 affirms, "Wives, submit yourselves unto your own husbands, as unto the Lord. For the husband is the head of the wife, even as Christ is the head of the church: and He is the savior of the body. Husbands, love your wives, even as Christ also loved the church, and gave Himself for it."

A husband who is the head of his household, will love his wife as Christ loved the church. He will pray for you, provide, protect, and love you. Submission honors God. There are women who have been married for years, but they are still not a wife. They are just a roommate. They refuse to honor their husband. They have the title, but don't function in the position as a wife.

As a wife, submission honors and affirms your husband's leadership, even as he affirms the gifts that you bring as a helpmate. Understand that if serving and submitting is above you, then marriage is below you. Submission doesn't mean control. Submission doesn't mean put a tether on somebody. Submission isn't manipulative or controlling, to where you become a private investigator to keep someone under surveillance. It doesn't even MapQuest their every move. Love doesn't restrain you from doing wrong, it constrains you to do right (2 Corinthians 5:14). You can't submit to any person, unless you submit to God first.

THE RIGHT RIB

I believe that a man knows he has found his rib, when he can breathe a lot easier. If he's stressing, suffering, or suffocating, then that may not be the right rib. Don't rush the process,

because you will always ruin what you rush. I'm learning

that it's better to wait long, than to marry wrong. Waiting on

God for the right one at the right time, is better than rushing

and wishing you waited.

STAY WOKE

I find it interesting that God asked Adam to name the

animals, but He didn't consult with Adam about how he

wanted his woman created. Adam was sleep. Here's a tip,

stop trying to wake up the man, that God is still working on.

If he's sleep and seemingly unconscious, then let him sleep.

He's sleeping on your value, because he's not the right

one for you. Stay woke, because God is sending a man

whose awakened by your aura, beauty, integrity, and vitality.

God created the woman so uniquely, that when Adam awoke

she made him holler and say, "Whoa man!" God knows how

to create what you want and give you, what you didn't even realize you needed. He knows what you have need of, before you even ask Him (Matthew 6:8).

God is the only one I know, who will give you a gift, that puts Him in competition for your attention. Think about it. Sometimes we pray real hard, before we get blessed. After we receive the blessing God has to say, "Hey don't forget about me over here." Adam eventually found himself, in a war with God the giver and Eve the gift. In Genesis chapter 3, Adam sinned against God as he followed Eve, by eating of the tree of knowledge of good and evil. Adam was split, between his relationship with God and his relationship with the one God created. You see, the man followed God and the woman followed the man. However, sin revered the order of God's order. The focus was flipped, to where the man followed the woman, but God doesn't follow anybody. You have to follow Him!

I don't care how much money they have. I don't care how fine you think he is, never abandon the giver for the gift. The gift can't give you God. Only God can give you the gift. Don't love the gift, more than you love the giver of the gift.

WIFE LIFE

Stop looking for it and let God give you it. Stop looking for a man and let God give you the right one, that will find you. Proverbs 18:22 declares, "Whoso findeth a wife findeth a good thing, and obtaineth favor of the Lord." Anything that's worth finding, is not easy to find. As a woman are you that "good thing" that's worth finding? You are the prize. You are the favor, that a man receives for his labor. You don't just become a wife, when you get married and march down the aisle, to say your vows. The Bible calls you a "wife" before a man finds you and marries you.

The term "wife" is more than a title, it's the life you

live. It's the way that you prepare yourself now, for what is to come. A ring doesn't mean anything, if the right man from God, doesn't put it on your finger. When you meet the right man, you won't have time to get ready. You will need to already be ready. Like they say, "If you stay ready, you won't have to get ready." God has what you want. It's ready for you, but are you ready for it? When everyone is going to happy hour, get happy and go to the gym. While everyone else is clubbing, learn how to perfect your cooking. When everyone is going out, stay in and build your business. When all the rest are surrounding themselves, with any and everybody, value your body.

Stop trying to fit, where you don't belong! Let God pick and select what you need. What you would choose, doesn't compare to the best choice God has for you. When the right man has you, he will say, "Whoa man! I thank God for blessing me, with a woman like you."

CHAPTER 3

No More Drama

*Life doesn't give you an Academy Award,
for being a drama queen.*

Y ou are too blessed to be stressed and associate

with people, who bring drama, junk, and mess. When you

really want better for your life, you will disassociate from

negative people, drama, and dream killers. You will never

live your best life, until you let go of anger, negativity,

bitterness, and strife.

Give all of it an eviction notice! You may not know

where it's going, but it can't stay here. It can't remain in your

mind, heart, and spirit. You have come too far, to stay where

you are. The argument isn't worth it. The backbiting and

fighting is a waste of your time. Cursing them out, is a waste of your breath and energy. Don't allow someone to put you in a bad light, because they don't want to see you shine.

DRAMA QUEEN

I've come to the realization, that some people are like soap operas, they're just filled with drama. Imagine if life, was like the *Academy Awards.* I'm sure you could think of somebody, who deserves the title of best actor or actress, because of all their drama. They are deserving of a *Daytime Emmy,* for all of the drama they keep up, day after day. However, life is not an award show. Life doesn't give you an *Academy Award* or *Emmy Award*, for being a drama queen. You know, some people just have to keep up mess. They have to put others down, to lift themselves up. They have to talk about people to you, in order to dump their nasty and negative junk on you. Realize though, if they talk about people to you, then they will talk about you to people. If they dog them out and bring you a bone of bitterness, they will take another bone and share your issues with someone else too.

If people are talking behind your back, that means you're already ahead of them. If they are trying to pull you down, that means they are already below you. Rise above the negativity. Keep your back to the past and your face to the future. For some people, nothing is right unless something is wrong. Stay away from drama queens and dream killers, who find something wrong with everything. Distance yourself from pessimistic people, because they will pollute the power in your spirit.

JEWELRY BOX

You are a jewel, stop letting people deposit and dump junk in your jewelry box. You have priceless pearls of peace and prosperity within you. Don't let someone dump trash in your treasure. Protect your jewels, because "The thief cometh not, but for to steal, and to kill, and to destroy" (John 10:10). Don't let a thief steal your jewels of joy. Don't let anyone kill your vibe. Don't allow anybody, to destroy your destiny. Hold fast to your treasure and let the trash go! As you let negative people go, you will see that drama leaves right along with them. Through it all, remember that God allows some people to walk out of your life, to make room for the right people to walk into your life. Trust the process, everything will work out for the best.

THE BLESSING OF LETTING GO

It's incumbent upon you, to press forward and not look back. Don't even run back, to place people back in your life that God removed out of your life. It's your job to let them go, so you can grow. Stop holding on to people, that have let you go. The drama is holding you, because you're holding it. Let it go! Give yourself room to bloom. Let go of negative people who are holding on to you, because they will hold you back from your destiny and purpose.

You can't do permanent things, with temporary people. Permanent things with temporary people, leaves permanent scars. Short term pleasure, is not worth long term pain. The place to begin living drama free, is to understand there is a blessing in this lesson of letting go. You have the patience, persistence, and preparation to pass the test. Bless and release who you need to, so you can walk in the place of blessing that God has for you.

IS LOVING THEM, HURTING YOU?

I know you think it's easier said than done. You've known the person for so many years. You love them. You genuinely care about their well-being and you just can't make the break, so quickly. However, is loving them, hurting you? Sometimes we stay where we are, because we don't believe we deserve better. If you don't take personal inventory of your relationships, you will slowly seep into a cesspool of negativity. You will ultimately drown in destruction.

Rid your life of toxic relationships. Eventually, they will destroy you and everything that's associated with you. When you think about it, you can either deal with the nagging pain of staying in an abusive, toxic, and hurtful relationship or make the sudden break. Either way, there will be pain. Yes, sometimes it hurts to let go. It hurts even more to hold on, when it's hurting you. Do you want the pain of regression or progression? Would you rather limp or leap?

THE GIFT OF GOODBYE

Realize that toxic relationships, are a biohazard to your breakthrough and blessings. Toxic connections and relationships are unhealthy, which will destroy your life. Toxic relationships, will not only cause you heartbreak and heartache, but heartburn and heart attack. They will make you bitter, when you were born to be better.

They say, "It's not what you walk away from, it's what you walk away with." Many of us have walked away from toxic relationships. However, we have also walked away with a broken heart, emotional baggage, scars of abuse, mistrust, depression, addiction, and low self-esteem. These were not parting gifts, but rather curses that will destroy your life and the generations to come. As a result of walking away, we walk right back into what we are used to. We leave toxic relationships, to get right back into similar ones that initially hurt us. We find ourselves with a new person, in a new relationship, but the same old situation.

CIRCLE OF SUCCESS

Sometimes we have become so numb to pain, that it hurts to be happy. So much so, that we become comfortable with sadness, rejection, lies, and wounds. As a result, we become callous and nonchalant. When our expectations and standards are lowered, we begin to speak out of our hurt. You may even find yourself saying to someone, "Leave if you want to. I've been hurt before anyway." Begin to renew your mind and heal from within. If you don't, then you will attract to you, the hurt that flows from you. Give yourself the gift of healing and forgiveness, to break the curse of bitterness and brokenness over your life. Forgive whoever hurt you and forgive yourself, for allowing it to happen. You will never get better, if you continue to remain bitter.

You don't need a whole bunch of people in your life, you just need the right people. The right people and relationships won't reduce you, they will produce greater purpose in you. Never reduce yourself, to fit in with people who don't like you anyway. The people who try to reduce you, can see in you what you don't see in yourself. They can see your purpose and potential. Their envy is enkindled. As a result, they will try to destroy you, so that you don't walk in your God-given greatness.

When God is for you, the "who" doesn't matter. When God favors you, people who don't like you can't do anything about it. Be cognizant of who is in your circle. Forge connections with people, who want to see you grow and get to the next level. Create a circle of success.

One of the most important decisions that you will ever make, are the relationships that you choose to align yourself with daily. Whether it be friendships, business, dating, or marriage, it will either reap fruitful or frightful results. Make sure the people who step into your life, have something to add to it and vice versa. Major dreamers, don't associate with dream killers and minor thinkers. Create a circle of go-getters and dream developers!

CANCEL MY SUBSCRIPTION, I'M THROUGH WITH YOUR ISSUES

As you read and mentally digest this wisdom, envision yourself in a greater place of peace and prosperity. Even now, the vision for your life is being restored. It's been suggested, "Having sight, without vision means you're still blind."

Do you believe there's more ahead for your life, than what has been? You are called to be greater, do greater things, and live on a greater level. You're far beyond the mediocre and mundane. There's more that you are to experience and achieve. Trust God and stay motivated through the process.

A negative state of mind, will trap you in a state of sickness, by suffocating your dreams and visions. When you get to a place that says, "I'm sick and tired, of being sick and tired," then you won't settle for mediocrity and mess. You will do more than survive, you will begin to thrive!

Begin to mentally break out of the box of brokenness. Start living, thinking, and moving freely. You have to walk in freedom, because you can't live aimlessly and void of purpose. Refuse to be sad, bad, and mad. Refuse to live your life, barely making it. You're too gifted, to have less and think less of yourself. Begin to live life more abundantly. You're too gifted, to be looking for a man to bail you out. Stir and develop your gifts. Free your mind. Don't waste your time and mental energy, by being angry about what didn't work or who didn't treat you right.

Stop subscribing to mental junk and issues that should be discarded! A junk filled mind, is worse than junk mail. Send negativity a notice that says, "Cancel my subscription, I'm through with your issues." I'm through with issues of jealousy, issues of strife, and issues that impede my life. Today it's officially over. Unsubscribe from unflattering thoughts about yourself. Unsubscribe from upheaval. Cancel every negative issue. Don't subscribe to mess, when you were born to live blessed! Extra! Extra! Read all about it! Cancel my subscription, I'm through with your issues!

ENEMY OR INNER-ME?

It's time to stop being your own worst enemy. It's time to become your best friend. For some of us, the greatest enemy can be the "inner-me," because of a negative self-concept identity. Low self-esteem will keep you in a state of regression, rather than progression. A positive state of mind, will usher you into the spectrum of success. Shut the door, draw a line in the sand, and announce that you will no longer be a liability. Your life will be an asset to somebody, even if the somebody is you!

Don't go negative on the negative. Stay positive in the negative situation, because breakthrough is on the way! Let's be real, yes we have been victims, but we have also been perpetrators. As long as this world revolves and spins around, what goes around will come back around.

It's funny how we judge people, when we are guilty ourselves. Keep your mouth off people. There is something that God can easily bring up, that would make you shut up. Yet He covered you, in order to help someone recover from the same thing you went through. The grace that you want extended to you, should be extended to others as well. Imagine what would happen, if you prayed for them as much as you talk about them? Don't allow the "inner-me" to become your enemy. Begin to walk in victory!

SHAKE IT OFF

If somebody was to write your life story, I'm sure there are some chapters you might want to leave out. There are some secret scars, that you don't want to talk about. I'm talking about the painful issues and mistakes, that you don't want anybody to even know about. So, like a pregnant woman with a child, you carry it. You nurse it and nurture the pain. Now it grows into grief, that you grapple with daily. When you stop grieving and groveling, God can begin releasing your blessing.

Secret hurts becomes shackles that cripple your life. Mental pains are more severe than metal chains. Shake off what is shackling you. Get that mess and stress, off your mind and out of your life. God is setting you free, from the secret pains you've harbored for years. Stop trying to keep alive, what was meant to die. Shake off sadness, depression, shame, insecurity, and thoughts of suicide. You shall not die. This is your time to live through it, because greater blessings will come out of it. Shake it off!

CREATE YOUR CREED

I don't watch movies much, but some time ago I saw the film *Creed*. The plot details a famous boxer's son, Adonis Creed, who motivates himself to overcome hurt and hurdles, to become a prize fighter.

While training, his coach Rocky said, "Look in the mirror. Your greatest opponent, is the one staring back at you." What do you see, when you look in the mirror? Do you see your weaknesses or strengths? Do you see the worst or the best in yourself? When you develop laserlike focus, then you begin to realize there are no opponents. It's just you against you.

Creed's greatest opponent, was not on the outside. His fiercest opponent, was on the inside. As I previously stated, the greatest enemy can often be the "inner-me." However, you have to dig deep and find determination within. The battle is in your mind. When you find victory on the inside, it will transform your world on the outside.

Nobody can stop you, but you. They may try to block you, but ultimately they can't stop you. Don't allow minor circumstances, to thwart your major dreams. Don't allow small obstacles, to prevent you from thinking BIG! The bigger your battle, the greater your breakthrough.

KEEP FIGHTING

Much like Adonis Creed, you have been fighting all of your life. Fighting hurt. Fighting rejection. Fighting critics. Fighting disappointment. Fighting against negative thinking. Despite the fight you face, you already have the victory because the fight is fixed! You may have been knocked down, but don't stay down. Rise and get back up again. A knockdown becomes a knockout, when you stay down. Get back in the fight!

In the movie, Rocky said, "It's not how hard you can hit. It's about how hard you can get hit and keep moving forward." Life has hit you with its best shot. You've been hit and hurt, but you're still standing!

Like most films, the director shoots the ending first and works the remaining scenes into the movie. Your life is a movie and you have a starring role in it. You're the star and nobody else, can play your role better than you. Surround yourself with people, who will be your best supporting actors and unwrap your unlimited potential. Don't let negative people, make a cameo appearance in your scenes of success. Don't allow them to play a role, in your life's movie.

God is the director of your life. He already determined your ending, before you were born. In the end you win! Everything around you may be broken, but the fight is fixed. You've already won, before the battle began. Don't give up, but look up. If you can look up, then you can get up!

So, what's your creed? What is your purpose, mission statement, and life message? What are you willing to fight for? Your creed is the engine and the cauldron, to ignite your determination, on the road to your destination. Your creed must become the motivation, for every deed. If all you have is a creed, but no deed, then you won't succeed. In essence, "Faith without works is dead" (James 2:26). You must back up your words, by putting in the work. The hustle and muscle is a key element to your greatness. Exercise your faith. Create a creed for healing, joy, peace, love, and life more abundantly! Work your creed and your creed will work for you.

THE BLESSING OF BEING BROKEN

There is a beauty and blessing in being broken. Sometimes being rejected, gets you connected back to God. As crazy as it sounds, you can literally be blessed by being broken. Mark chapter 6 details the story of Jesus feeding 5,000 people, with just 5 loaves and 2 fish. Now mathematically this is impossible, because there's just not enough food for everybody. However, when Jesus is in the mix, nothing is impossible. Even the laws of math don't matter.

Before Jesus disseminated the 5 loaves and 2 fish, He blessed it and broke it. The more He broke it, the more people were able to be nourished by it. Now the laws of math would suggest that 5 loaves multiplied by 2 fish, can never feed 5,000 people. However, Jesus continually divided the food among the people.

The more that you've been broken, the more pieces of your life you're able to share, to strengthen somebody else. God will mend your life, to where you can find peace from broken pieces. He can create greatness from a great mess.

Never discount yourself and doubt that you're blessed. Despite the breaking, God will use every situation to birth your breakthrough and blessing. The breaking is a setup for greater blessing. The anointing on your life, will not flow without you being broken. The pressure is necessary to prepare you, for where He's taking you. God will multiply your gifts, talents, and resources to bless others in the process. He can take what's not enough and make it more than enough.

God gave you a gift, so use it! Refuse to let people

steal your joy, serenity, and strength. The adversity was meant to break you, but God will bless and sustain you despite the situation. Get up, shake yourself, and get back in the fight. Break out of the box and bless the world, with everything that God gave you. You may be broken, but you can still breakthrough and break out, because you're blessed!

The world is waiting for you, to reveal the best of everything that's inside of you. Blast past your past. What's ahead of you, is far greater than anything that is behind you. Move forward and break out!

NO MORE PAIN, NO MORE GAMES

Mary J. Blige the Queen of Hip Hop Soul, recorded the commercially successful song, *No More Drama*, which was birthed out of her own personal pain. Any listener can hear Mary's message in the music, filled with passion and a desire to be free.

A musician once said, "Sometimes you have to get hit, to make a hit." A powerful thought to consider and maybe just maybe, you have to get broken, to write a book. Indeed your pain, often becomes the greatest poetry and remedy to life's malady. The song, *No More Drama* begins with the lyrics, "Broken heart again. Another lesson learned. Better know your friends or else you will get burned. Gotta count on me, cause I can guarantee that I'll be fine." How many broken relationships and disappointments have you experienced, that left your heart broken again? The lessons can either make us, wiser or weaker.

ISSUES, IT'S YOU

God was convinced of the greatness He placed in you, when He created you. God wants you to know about the riches He put in you, before your mother ever conceived you. Jeremiah 1:5 declares, "Before I formed thee in the belly I knew thee; and before thou camest forth out of the womb I sanctified thee." God wants you to know, what He knows about you. In order to find out, you have to inquire within, through His word. Seek ye first. Stop seeking them and start seeking Him. The problem is you're taking your problems to people, who already have problems of their own. You can't tell your problems to everybody, because 20% don't care and 80% are glad you have them. I believe that's 100%.

Take your issues and problems, to the problem solver. God has healing tissues, for every hurting issue. Keep saying the word "issues" enough and it will turn into "it's you." Analyze the person in the mirror. Stop allowing people to be your crutch and discover the power of you, in you. Stop relying on people out of desperation, so you can find the inspiration and motivation within. The right people won't burn you, they will bless you. They will love you, even when everyone else walks out on you. Yes, you can count on

God. However, the person you must also be able to count on, is the one in the mirror.

DESTINY OVER DRAMA

The soul in Mary J. Blige's voice, seems to soothe the struggle that she sings about. In the song she says, "It feels so good, when you let go of all the drama in your life. Now you're free from all the pain. Free from all the games. Free from all the stress. So find your happiness."

You have to make a decision to walk in your destiny, rather than live a life of drama. This is the day, where you become allergic to average. No more average relationships, that make you sick and suffocate your success. No more tears about the past. No more crying every night. No more confusion. No more heartache. No more animosity and anger. No more trials and tribulations. No more pain. No more games. No more drama. Show drama, bitterness, and strife to the exit door out of your life! Mary ends the song by expressing, "It's up to us to choose, whether we win or lose and I choose to win." The question is, will you choose to do the same? Being happy and discovering joy is a choice!

I can't twist your arm to be happy and find joy. You have to want it and decide to live in it. A life that's fulfilling, is a life worth living. You need peace of mind and you can choose to find happiness, in the midst of hardship. Walk away from drama and begin to walk in your destiny!

CHAPTER 4

Cover Girl

A made up mind, is more important than a made up face.

In 1997, *CoverGirl* cosmetics launched what is now the famous slogan, "Easy, breezy, beautiful *CoverGirl*." The commercialization of the cosmetic chain, painted a vivid picture of a "girl-next-door" type of look. The marketing for their makeup line, has showcased celebrities such as Drew Barrymore, Queen Latifah, Taylor Swift, Janelle Monáe, and Rihanna.

While seeking to portray, the "girl-next-door" image, *CoverGirl's* commercials never actually used the everyday "girl-next-door." Imagine how compelling the commercials would be, if the woman on the screen was from the same community, had the same career, and dealt with the same issues as you. I think their marketing team, should consult with me. Nevertheless, *CoverGirl* uses models, singers, and entertainers, who are only an infinitesimally small part of the population. Isn't it interesting when people, who aren't in the same situations you're experiencing, try to portray how you should feel and look.

The best *CoverGirl* model, is the woman who is reading this book. You don't have to be a supermodel. You are a superwoman, who soars above obstacles. Your beauty is dependent on how you base it, not how society paints it. Even when your face wasn't made up, you had a made up mind to make it. The best makeup that a woman can wear, is the smile on her face. You're a divine depiction, of how to dance into your destiny. You're a spokeswoman, for transforming stumbling blocks into stepping stones. You're a role model that conveys and portrays what success looks like, despite scars. No one can truly understand your hustle, if they haven't been in your struggle. A made up mind, is more important than a made up face.

EASY, BREEZY, BEAUTIFUL

If only what you went through in life was as easy, breezy, and beautiful as a *Covergirl* commercial. If you've been where I've been in life, then you can most assuredly agree that you've endured some tough stuff. The tempestuous winds you had to face. The ugly situations you smiled through, isn't for the faint of heart. Life has been anything but easy, breezy, and beautiful for you. However, the pain birthed the champion inside of you.

It should have been easy, but you faced hard times. Life should have been sunny and breezy, but you experienced stormy and windy times. Everything should have been as beautiful as you are, but certain situations got ugly. Yet you persevered through the high winds, high water, and hellish hurricanes of life. I know it wasn't easy, but it was worth it. Don't let the negative of what you went through, get in you. Allow God's power to cover and fill you. What you went through doesn't define you, it refines you. You're stronger today, because of what you endured yesterday.

WHAT'S UNDER THE COVER?

The word "cover" means to put something on top or in front of, in order to protect and conceal it. How many times have you concealed and covered your emotions, to protect your heart? You perfumed your pain, masked it with makeup, and concealed it with concealer. Due to hurt, pain, rejection, and isolation you developed barriers, to shield yourself from those with bad intentions. We have all had our heart and spirit crushed, in some way shape or form. Even still, God can transform the situation and give us determination.

You have covered your face with makeup, not only to enhance your appearance, but to diminish the agony. You covered the hurt, by surrounding yourself with associates and friends. In a crowd of people, but you still felt lonely. You covered it by dressing your best on the outside, but you were still a mess on the inside. You covered the pain with success, but you still didn't feel your best.

Even now God is covering you, despite all that you've been through. Jesus said, "Come unto me, all ye that labor and are heavy laden, and I will give you rest" (Matthew 28:11). Essentially, if you give God your hardship, He will give you healing. You have been toiling. You have been tired. It's time to find tranquility. If you trust God through the test, He will give you rest.

TAKE OFF THE MASK AND MASCARA

Makeup illuminates your face on the outside, but it does

nothing for the way you feel on the inside. You can't put makeup, over a messed up mindset. Something is wrong when superficiality, becomes the substratum of our foundation in society. Many would rather flaunt with a façade to smile on the outside, yet in reality they are depressed and discombobulated on the inside.

Far too often, we put on a fake smile, to hide real pain. Truth be told, we often hide behind what we possess on the outside, to cover-up what we're void of on the inside. All of the makeup in the world, can't cover a sad soul. The blush can't brush away the pain. You wear hair bundles and *Remy* extensions, but your life is a bundle of brokenness. Sadly, we put more effort into what goes on our head, rather than what goes in our head. Place your hand in the hands of the One, who knows the number of hairs on your head.

For far too long, you have masked your issues with makeup. Perfumed your pain. Deodorized the funk of your issues. If you presently continue to live in the past, it will offset the blessings of your future. Oftentimes, we have become desensitized, to believing that the more things we buy, the more friends we have, and the more money we accumulate will alleviate the void in our lives. The false narrative, will never become a true reality. You have to get real, with the real you.

MASK OFF

What you don't reveal, can never be healed. The title "Mask Off" is more than a song, from the rapper Future. It addresses the plight of your past and the state of your future. What good is it to have a made up face, but a messed up mind? A pretty face plus an ugly attitude, just makes you a pretty ugly person. Despite the ugly scars of life, you can still find beauty from brokenness. True beauty, never originates from the outside-in, it always derives from the inside-out.

What are you dealing with internally? How long has it

been going on? When will you release it? Your tears have

stained the pages, as you think about the stages of your life.

No, each day hasn't been dismal, but the pain seems to last

longer than the joy. So many times we hide behind a mask, to

mask the past. Take off the mask and begin to look within,

the mirror of your soul. Many times we're afraid to address

issues within, because it brings up old memories, scars, and

wounds from the past. The wounds are a portal to your

wisdom. Your devastation becomes elevation, for your

empowered purpose.

How can you heal from it, if you won't deal with it?

How can you address, what you won't confess? Stop going

through life numb and on auto-pilot. You will never move

forward, if you keep living your life in reverse. Take control

of your life. Get in the drivers seat and press forward on the

road to your destiny. Oftentimes, what you are without

begins from within. The outside won't fix the inside, until you deal with what's on the inside first. When you work on yourself from within, the true beauty of you will shine through.

FORGIVE TO LIVE

What do you do, with the hurt and pain that you have experienced? Do you hold on to it? Do you release it? Are you bitter or better because of it? The writer Mark Twain said, "Forgiveness is the fragrance, that the violet sheds on the heel that has crushed it."

How do you respond when you've been crushed, by life's crippling trials? There is a choice that you must make, to either release it or hold on to it. Holding it will hurt you, releasing it will heal you. It's just that simple. You say, "Well, it's not that simple. You don't understand, but they did this." Okay, but what will you do now? Move forward and tap into the power of forgiveness. It's over. Whatever happened in the past is over. Forgiveness shuts the door on your past and opens the door to your future!

How long will you live as a victim? Move from victim to victory! Living presently in the past, stifles the blessings of your future. You may be hurting, but you have hurt others too. Break the cycle, because hurting people hurt other people. Bitterness becomes an emotional cancer, that destroys you from the inside out. Stop carrying around emotional baggage. It's weighing down your self-esteem, mindset, peace, and lifestyle. You can't truly live, until you forgive!

FORGIVENESS IS FREEDOM

I'm a living witness that forgiveness is freedom. When you don't forgive someone it doesn't hurt them, it hurts you. Forgive whoever hurt you and forgive yourself, for allowing it to happen. You will never get better, until you stop being bitter! Forgiveness is freedom. It shuts the door on your past and opens the door to your future! Forgive and move forward by any means necessary!

Take the time to pause and ponder, by doing a personal life assessment. Simply think. What are you holding on to that's stifling your growth? Holding on to the past is a hazard and hindrance, to your happiness and hope. There are some people that you have to bless and release, from your life. Some people that we connected to, were not good to or for us and we knew that. However, we decided to connect with those individuals anyway and got hurt in the process. You can't be free for your future, if you're bound by your past. Yes, we have been victims, but we have also been perpetrators, of our own behavior. If God forgave you, then forgive yourself and forgive others. Seek to forgive and seek to be forgiven.

10 - 90

I came across a quote that suggests, "Life is 10% what happens to you and 90% how you react to it." Everybody will go through something in life. So, it's not solely about what you go through. It's about how you handle, what you go through.

What do you do, when you experience tragedy that you can't seem to get over? The childhood abuse, the rape, the divorce, or the betrayal. Will you focus on the 10% or the 90%?

Oftentimes, 90% of the time, we dwell on the 10% that has happened to us. The abuse, rejection, pain, mistakes, and abandonment is only a small percentage of your life. What will you do, with the resounding remaining percentage? As we say, "Stop hustling backwards." Don't allow 10% to control 100% of your life. Begin to flip your focus, in a forward direction of progression, not recalcitrant regression. To forge ahead, you have to forgive and move past anything, that has kept you behind. Make a decision that each day you won't be bitter, but you will strive to be better.

RECOVER GIRL

You've tried to cover up the abuse, the shame, torment, trials, and tribulations. You can't heal from it, until you deal with it. When you uncover it and reveal it, then surely God can heal you from it. The memory will now become a testimony. Your misery will become your ministry. Your mess will become your message. Your stumbling block, will become a stepping stone. God will use your setback, as a set up for your greatest comeback. Your life will become living proof, that God can use your tragedy as strategy to rise to higher heights.

Your mental health and peace of mind, are essential for longevity of life. The right people can also assist you, in the process of personal peace. Licensed and trained professionals such as counselors, psychologists, and health practitioners are often necessary for our personal growth and development. We can't continue to view therapy as taboo. At times, it's necessary for me and you.

Recognize your value and know your worth! Don't let the valuables on you, outweigh the value in you. Take off the mask and unveil the real you. Don't live your life, as a second rate version of yourself, when you were born to be a first class woman. You're pregnant with purpose, promise, and possibility. Now is the time, to give birth to your destiny and press past the obstacles, that have held you back.

When you get a mental and spiritual makeover, it will radiate through your physical pulchritude and outward beauty. When you transform your mind, your entire world will be transformed.

Inner beauty radiates more than makeup, self-love

outshines any designer shoe, and inner healing is more priceless than a handbag. Love, nurture, and value the greatness that is within you. There is more joy, peace, love, and happiness that awaits you. You don't have to be a cover girl, you are a covered girl. God covered you, through the storm, stress, and mess to declare you blessed. Take off the superficial mask and begin to love the real you!

Allow God's power to cover you, so He can overshadow you. As God covers you, He will recover the joy you lost. You will recover from the broken relationship. You will recover from a broken heart. You will recover from the financial loss. You will recover from abuse. You will recover from divorce. You will recover from sickness and walk in healing. You will recover from brokenness and find breakthrough. You will recover from every wound and discover wisdom. You will recover because you are an overcomer!

CHAPTER 5

Love Yourself

You can't expect anybody to love you,
if you don't love yourself.

I f you don't love yourself, someone will come along and show you how to hate yourself. As a result, you will ascribe to their philosophy internally and transmit that negativity to others.

It's true that you can't expect anybody to love you, if you don't love yourself. How do you love yourself, if you've never had love expressed to you? How do you express love, if you've never seen an example of it? These days, the word "love" seems to just be a feel good phrase, a tattoo on someone's arm, a heart emoji when you text, or a hashtag to search on social media. However, very few find it in real life.

Love seems to be lifeless and meaningless, because so many people have abused it in a reckless manner.

Do you love someone how they need to be loved, or do you love them based on how you decide to love? How do you know how to love someone, if they don't know how they need to be loved themselves? It's something to ponder and consider. This is the unique dichotomy of love, in the matrix of relationships.

Love is just a word, if there is no action associated with it. In fact, the word "love" demands a response expressed through actions. The Bible says, "For God so loved the world, that He gave" (John 3:16). If you notice, God's action of loving, is followed by giving. You can give without loving, but you can't love without giving. Don't confuse giving, with only receiving something tangible.

I know when you go on a date to dinner or a movie, he will PAY for you. However, does he PRAY with and for you too? Don't get so blinded by tangible things, that you fail to see intangible attributes and qualities. You can't put a price on someone giving their time, compassion, consideration, encouragement, respect, support, or even treating you like a queen. Don't take them for granted, because you can't find that quality of person everywhere. You may think chivalry is dead, but a real gentleman always keeps it alive. Holding doors, holding hands, and holding your heart with tender loving care is in his DNA.

FREE YOURSELF

Free yourself from anxiety, bitterness, and negativity. The power of forgiveness frees you, from strife and mess. You love yourself by freeing yourself. When you really love yourself, you don't stay attached to people who debilitate you. When you love yourself, you don't hold grudges and continue to think negatively. Your past is a prison, but your future is freedom,

Don't allow a bad relationship, abuse, haters, financial woes, addiction, or depression to keep you bound. The bitterness of being bound, will eat away at your health and peace of mind. Being bitter will keep you stressed, but getting better makes you blessed! Love yourself enough, to let it go. Bitterness, anger, animosity, and revenge is like picking up a hot coal, to throw it at the person who hurt you. However, you got burned before it left your hand! When you don't free yourself and forgive somebody, it doesn't hurt them. It hurts you! It takes more work and hardship to get even, than it does to forgive. Let it go, before you go too far. If God can forgive you of what you have done, then surely He can forgive them and empower you to forgive too. Free yourself for yourself!

IT'S EN VOGUE

The sultry and sophisticated female singing group En Vogue, was one of the premiere voices of the 1990s. The group had a chart topping song, "Free Your Mind." The lyrics conveyed said, "Before you can read me, you gotta learn how to see me. Free your mind and the rest will follow." As you know, artists and singing groups come and go. They can be famous today and infamous tomorrow. However, En Vogue understood a key principle and that is, a free mind can never go out of style.

The first black President of South Africa, Nelson Mandela, was great because he forgave. He was a man of peace, in a time of war. In an age of apathy, Mandela took action. As a political activist, he opposed a government that inflicted violence, on its people. He challenged the archaic ideologies of injustice. As a result, Mandela was sent to prison on Robben Island for 27 years, by the apartheid white government. Can you imagine 27 years in confinement, being incarcerated, and isolated? Mandela was separated from his home, his wife, and his children. During his time of imprisonment, Mandela was forbidden from attending his own mother's funeral. He was also not allowed, to attend the funeral of his son, who was killed in a car accident.

Mandela spent his most productive years incarcerated, as a political prisoner. Many of our brothers and sisters, know what being locked up feels like. Here in America, which is incarceration nation, black/brown men and women are disproportionately warehoused in prisons. Many are given harsh sentences and incarcerated, based on non-violent offenses. On the contrary, many of their counterparts of other races are given little to no time, for the same crimes.

Imagine the anger that they feel, even the anger that Mandela harbored. It's one thing to be angry, it's another thing to stay angry. It's one thing to be mad, but it's another thing to make a difference. If anybody should have stayed angry, it should have been Mandela because he was incarcerated unjustly. However, Mandela didn't allow Robben island, to rob him of the power to forgive. He decided to make a difference. In 1994, Mandela became the first black president of South Africa, at the age of 75. Mandela brought reconciliation to a nation. Regardless of your stage or age, it's not too late to be great, neither is it too early to get started. This is why Mandela could say, "It always looks impossible, until it's done."

No matter how difficult it seems to be, continue to push forward with faith. Lead with love and overcome every obstacle. Adjust your vision, to see every *Impossible* as *I'm Possible*. Find the *Can* in every *Can't* and grow through every situation. Before he was granted freedom, Mandela found freedom in prison.

Some people are in a psychological prison without

bars. The chains and shackles are not metal, but they're mental. Mandela freed his mind, which opened the door to his freedom. How many doors have been closed, because your mind was locked up? You can't expect to achieve your unlimited dreams, with a limited mindset. A closed mind, will never open BIG doors. Free your mind from the prison of your past, so you can walk boldly into your future.

It's about more than your three snaps and a neck roll. More than your beauty, encompassed by your hips and lips. More than you pulling up to the scene, with your ceiling missing. More than you rocking your stunner shades. More than you going on a girls trip, with your sorority sisters. More than you having a ring on your finger and a man on your arm. Life is about more than you being able to slay, with your designer bag and heels. It's about more than you having your hair whipped, dipped, fried, dyed, and laid to the side. You know what's really en vogue? Being free, healed, and empowered to empower somebody else.

LIVE IN LOVE

I've learned that you have to forgive people, who may never give you an apology. Forgiveness is not only, for the one who hurt you. It's for you, so you can stop hurting over what was done to you. Hurting people will hurt people, but only healed people can walk in healing.

Doctors and therapists have linked bitterness to diseases, sicknesses, and a lack of unity in relationships. Bitterness will kill you and everything around you, from the inside-out. You can't keep holding on to something, that's killing you. If you eat unhealthy foods, you will be an unhealthy person. If you hold grudges, you will be a bitter person. If you connect to negative people, it will corrupt your positive mindset.

Bitterness is a thief and it steals your joy, happiness,

and longevity of life. John 10:10 affirms, "The thief cometh not, but for to steal, and to kill, and to destroy: I am come that they might have life, and that they might have it more abundantly." I always wondered, why did Jesus say "might have." Why didn't He use the words "will have?" Simply because He already gave you life, but the question is what will you do with it? I can't make you take a pair of shoes, if you don't want them. I can't make you receive something that you don't want. If you take it and don't want it, then you will put it back when I turn my back. Jesus already died, but it's up to you to live. You have to want life and walk in it abundantly, when every situation around you is designed to produce death. It's easy to give up and die, but it's hard to live.

To live is a choice. To live means, I'm in a battle between the old man and the new man. To live means, I'm fighting off my past to walk in my future. To live means, I will forgive when I have every reason not to. To live means, I will have the victory and live abundantly. When you forgive somebody, you're not setting them free. You're setting yourself free! Let it go and free yourself, because it's not worth the stress. I've got news for you, your blood pressure will go down if you forgive. Your hair will stop falling out, if you forgive. Your stress will decrease, if you forgive. Your attitude will take you to a higher altitude, if you forgive. You'll stop cursing, being mean, nasty and evil, if you forgive. Begin to live in love! You will set yourself free from, anger, wrath, bitterness, and strife when forgiveness becomes a part of your life.

UNCLOG YOUR DRAIN

It doesn't take a plumber to know, that you can't operate a drain that's clogged. Nothing will flow through it, until the junk is removed from it. Nothing good will flow to you, until negativity flows out of you. You're a jewel, so don't allow junk to rot your soul and spirit. You don't even look happy or feel good about yourself, because the junk of this world has clogged your spirit. As a result, you're now expressing on the outside, what you feel on the inside.

People who don't feel good about themselves, find ways to make others feel bad about themselves. They have to find a way, to find fault in others. They have to give somebody a piece of their mind. More than likely, that's probably all they have left is a piece, but no peace within. They curse, fuss, and fight because nothing internally is right. Don't allow junk to entrap your jewel within. Don't allow trash, to surround and suffocate your treasure. Unclog your drain of determination and pipe of peace, so that blessings can flow to you without any hindrance from you.

Just like you cleanse your body with water, begin to cleanse your heart and mind with God's Word, so that He can renew, refresh, refill, and reinvigorate your life. Free yourself, from the junk that hides the jewel in you.

The love that you're seeking on the outside, will never be actualized until you're healed and filled, with love on the inside. Love doesn't come to take, love comes to give. As a woman you are unique, extraordinarily special, and designed with a purpose in mind. You are worthy of love. You are beautiful and valuable in God's sight. When you love God, He shows you how to love yourself.

RESTORE IN PROGRESS

A while ago, I had some problems with my iPhone, due to losing data abruptly. My phone just went blank. My notes, contacts, and messages were all gone. Just poof, vanished! If you've been there, then you know how frustrating it is to lose your information.

So, I drove to the Apple Store and talked to one of the

Apple Genius workers about my issue. The guy ran a

diagnostic test on my phone and wondered, if I had my

computer with me. As a matter of fact, I did that day. He

walked to the back of the store and brought me a USB cord.

The guy calmly said, "We should be able to retrieve your

data, since your phone is backed up to your computer."

I remember thinking and saying to myself, "Should? You

better put every comma, period, contact, and message back

on my phone, with as much as I paid for it." Since he's a

genius, I need him to make my phone work in a genius way.

So, the guy instructs me to plug one side of the USB

cord into my phone and the other side of the cord into my

computer. As I'm waiting, I'm praying and crossing my

fingers, hoping that this issue gets resolved. All of a sudden,

a message flashes across the phone and it says, "Restore in

progress." In the midst of my phone activation, I got a

spiritual revelation. God is the computer, you are the phone, and Jesus is the cord. The cord was the restorative mediator and method, to transfer the content from the computer, back to my phone. I needed the cord to mediate the restoration of my phone. You need the grace and power of Jesus, who is the mediator to restore your life. Scripture affirms in I Timothy 2:5 "For there is one God, and one mediator between God and men, the man Christ Jesus."

In John 14:6, Jesus declared, "I am the way, the truth, and the life: no man cometh unto the Father, but by me." You can't be restored without Jesus or forgiven without Him. Only God's love, can restore your self-esteem and joy in life. He can restore your love. He can restore your hope. He can restore your vision. He can restore your family. You may have an iPad, iPod or an iPhone, but do you have "iPray, iLove, and iForgive?" If you don't, then you will live in your situation rather than walk in restoration. Despite the stress and mess, you will not regress. You will progress into a place of restoration. No looking back or going back! Oh and by the way, I got all my data back!

WHAT'S YOUR LOVE LANGUAGE?

There is a law of attraction and there is also a law, for one's love language. As you listen to what people say, also listen to what they don't say. What is their conversation absent and void of? If they communicate hate, negativity, and gossip then you can clearly hear that it's void of love. Whatever you're thinking and speaking, will eventually dictate where you're going. Your words create your world and what you speak into the atmosphere, will eventually appear. What you confess, will determine what you do or don't possess. If you continue to say that you're a failure or you can't achieve, then you never will. Proverbs 18:21, declares "Death and life are in the power of the tongue." Begin to develop your love language. Begin to confess and profess, that you will have the best.

A statement I often hear, "There are no good men out here." Maybe, you're not attracted to the ones who are good men. Why is it that you're not attracting the ones, who are good men? It's interesting, that some ladies will choose a "bad boy" over a good man. They would rather deal with a problem, than a solution. How can you get upset when you don't have a good relationship, with a "bad boy?" Your mama told you he was bad. His mama told you he was bad. As a matter of fact, the "bad boy" even told you, that he was bad himself. You just had to have, what you had to have. What could you possibly expect? Stop trying to fix him and transform a grown bad boy, into a good man. It won't work.

Could it also be that your mate is in the "friend zone?" Maybe you keep rejecting, who God keeps sending. Occasionally, I hear women say, "Well, he's just too nice." Really? I thought you wanted a gentleman. Someone who can build a family with you. A man who respects and treats you like a queen. I thought you wanted a man with a vision, not some false media depiction. Some women say, "Well he's just not my type." Again, maybe your type is the reason why you're single. See, you're intent on getting the type, that's not the right type for you. Start preparing for your prototype, not just the type you want. Oftentimes, what you want is really not what you need. What you're choosing, is not the best choice for you. Stop looking and start preparing. Let God prepare you, for the prototype that He has for you.

Beyond your beauty and voluptuous behind, what is the state of your mind? Your character will get, what your curves can't keep. Your standards will take you, where your body can't keep you. Don't lower them. Keep your standards higher than your heels and you will go to higher heights. Value you and love yourself. Let words of life, gauge your love language and life.

CHAPTER 6

Glow Up

You can never glow, where you refuse to grow.

The Creator of the universe who aligned the stars, had a purpose in mind for you to shine. When you work on yourself from within, the true beauty in you will shine through. Love, joy, and peace that radiates from you, will do for you what no makeup, earrings, heels, nails, or handbags could ever do.

The renowned Rev. Dr. Martin Luther King, Jr. declared, "Darkness cannot drive out darkness, only light can do that." You can look on the news, in your neighborhood, in your school, and realize that we're living in dark times. We are truly living in troubled times, and it seems as if there's a dark cloud hanging over our world. We're literally living in a generation, as II Timothy 3:2 declares, "For men shall be lovers of their own selves, covetous, boasters, proud, blasphemers, disobedient to parents, unthankful, unholy, trucebreakers, and without natural affection for one another." So void of natural affection, that a mother who gave birth to her children, can put those same children that came from her womb in a freezer to die. Seems like it's back to the future, because hate, racism, and vitriolic rage is in full bloom. We're living in times that people don't value your life, much less their own and will kill you over a pair of gym shoes or Cartier frame glasses.

We have perverse leaders void of principles. Since they can't keep it real, all they give us is fake news as their lips drip with the words of interposition and nullification. We have guided missiles, but misguided men. Money for bombs, but not books. Resources for war, but won't feed the poor.

They will close schools, but keep the prisons open. Slavery is under a new name, with a new Jim Crow. The ever increasing incarceration of black brothers and sisters, is at a disproportionate rate in these divided states of America.

Now the question becomes, how do you maintain a dream, when you're living in a nightmare? Seems like every other block, in inner city America has blight. Those who have much, continue to take from the have nots. We have more weed stores than grocery stores. So essentially, people get high but their life is still low. How do you maintain hope, when you're seemingly living in hopeless communities, during hopeless times?

GLOW IN THE DARK

There is a hopeless haze, hanging over our communities. In many cases, it's a microcosm of the dark cloud hanging over these yet to be United States of America. Yet still, the darker this world gets, the brighter you must shine.

One writer declared, "It's far better to light a candle, than to scream at the darkness." Yes indeed, we have to get to a place, where we do more than talk about how dark it is in the world. Rather, we have to flip the switch on. You and I have to turn on the light.

What good is it to be connected and plugged into an outlet in a dark room, but there's no light when you flick the switch? David the Psalmist declared, "Thy word is a lamp unto my feet and a light unto my path" (Psalm 119:105). When God lights your pathway, you will be able to know that the steps of a good man/woman are ordered by the Lord (Psalm 37:23).

No matter the darkness that surrounds you, God's light must shine through you. For greater is He (that being the light of Christ) that is in you, than he that is in the world (I John 4:4). God has given you power to turn the situation, the community, and this world right side up when things are

upside down.

SALT AND LIGHT

Scripture declares in Matthew 5:13, 14 "You are the salt

of the earth and the light of the world." Now, I'm sure you

know that salt makes food taste better. If I took you to dinner,

I would surely be able to find out, how much you like salt.

Well, the song did say, "Shake it like a salt shaker." I digress!

Some people's temperature is rising and blood pressure is

sky rocketing, because they use too much salt.

However, salt has some good properties in the process

of preserving the quality of food. Just like salt, God has

given you the power, to preserve your environment and make

things better. The reason your children aren't acting crazy,

because you are salt. The reason harm doesn't come your

way, because you're the salt of the earth. The reason the boss

can't treat you any kind of way, because your prayer life is the salt that preserves your house, spouse, career, community, finances, and family. You see, being salty ain't so bad after all!

Salt is about more than what you put on your food, it's what you add to your faith. Yes, salt makes food taste better, but being the salt of the earth should make you act better, pray harder, and believe greater for God to do something new right now.

See what good is a salt shaker, if the contents remain in the container? What good is your faith, if you don't use it? What good is the Gospel, if you don't share it. What good is the light, if you don't walk in it? As long as you're connected to the Savior, you can never lose your savor.

WHAT ARE YOU AFRAID OF?

Maurice Freehill declared, "Who is more foolish, the child afraid of the dark or the man afraid of the light?" Who is more foolish, the child that is afraid and fears the unknown or the adult that is afraid of truth, refusing to come into the light and lives in darkness? God has called you out of the shadows and into the light. Darkness and fear will paralyze you, but only the light of faith will mobilize you. Psalm 27 declares, "The Lord is my light and my salvation; whom shall I fear? The Lord is the strength of my life; of whom shall I be afraid?" So who and what are you afraid of? God already gave you salvation and strength. Even in dark times you can still shine, because the light of Christ is in you.

Stop being scared to shine. People will talk about you whether you fail or succeed. You might as well give it your all and soar to the stratosphere of success. Let them keep complaining and critiquing, you just keep succeeding and creating your best life.

VERTICAL AND HORIZONTAL

The light in you, should shine on somebody else too. You can't say you have fellowship with God, but won't have fellowship with me. How can you speak to God, but won't speak to somebody else? How can you speak in tongues, but then curse me out in English? Lord have mercy! You can't have a vertical relationship with God and not have a horizontal one with your brother or sister, who is made in the image of God. You can't say that you love a God you haven't seen but you're mean, nasty, bitter, and hateful to someone who you see every day. You can't be a hater of people and a lover of God, at the same time.

GROW UP AND GLOW UP

In order to shine and walk in the light, you have to grow up in order to glow up. The Apostle Paul declared, "When I was a child, I spake as a child, I understood as a child, I thought as a child: but when I became a man, I put away childish things" (I Corinthians 13:11). You have the form of masculinity. You have the outward adornment of femininity, but what is it without maturity and responsibility? It's not about your age, it's about your stage of maturity that makes the difference.

You have to mature and endure the growing pains of adversity, to shine in the light of opportunity. The problem is, everybody wants to shine and glow up. However, very few want to grow up. So many people, want to be on a stage that they are not ready to step on. They want the glitz, glamour, and glory but haven't endured the test to have a story. Don't allow your mind to be conformed, use God's Word and be transformed. You can never glow, where you refuse to grow.

ONE NIGHT ONLY

Despite the pain and the tears, understand that "Weeping may endure for a night, but joy is coming in the morning" (Psalm 30:5). If you can just get through the night. If you can get through the dark places, the sickness, the haters, the betrayal, and the adversity. If you can just get through the night, you will see the light on the other side! I don't know how long your night will last. I don't know how long the season of suffering will endure, but I do know it will end.

My weeping lasted for two years, each and every night as I battled to find the CAN in cancer. Through chemotherapy, radiation, hair loss, doubters, negative thoughts, and spinal taps I refused to lose. Yes, cancer made me cry, but it didn't make me quit. I can rejoice today, because God healed me and my life became a testimony of how to shine in dark times.

THIS TOO SHALL PASS

Whatever you're going through, just know that you're going

through and coming out stronger than when you went in. This too shall pass. The sickness shall pass. The struggle shall pass. The heartache shall pass. The loneliness shall pass. The trials and tribulation shall pass. The storm won't last. The struggle is over in your life!

STAY LIT

Do you realize, a candle that lights another candle never loses its flame? You've got it twisted because you think by giving, you're losing. No, it's a setup to begin receiving. Can your power still shine through, when it's dark around you? See, when you know what it's like to have the lights cut off, you can do like Teddy Pendergrass and light a candle.

I'm wondering, can you be a candle in the cave? I know the darkness is around you, but don't allow it to get in you. Nothing is so wrong, that you can't make it right. Nothing is so dark, that you can't bring the light. Move from darkness to light. Transition from ignorance to knowledge. Graduate from weakness to strength. Don't dim your light because of the darkness around you. Make it brighter and shine greater. No matter how dark and gloomy life becomes, the S-O-N is still shining and you've overcome. Only light can drive out darkness and only love can drive out hate. Remain focused on the light. Don't give up and don't quit. Just stay lit!

DISCERNMENT IN DARK TIMES

When you have eyes of faith, you can see a brighter day in the midst of a dark situation. Pray that God will give you discernment, so you can be aware of negative people, who seek to remove the positivity from your spirit. Some people are so negative, that you need to put them in a dark room to develop. Keep shining anyway and glow in the dark.

The longer you live, the brighter you must shine.

God will put a light inside of you, that no darkness around you can put out. Your bright future, is greater than your dark past. You may be disillusioned, distressed, depressed, and discouraged. Your situation may look dark, dismal, and desolate, but God will deliver you despite the darkness that surrounds you. As salt, you will never lose your savor, as long as you're connected to the Savior. Your light can never dim, as long as you're connected to Him.

TURN ON THE LIGHT

Sometimes it looks like God has hid you, but remember He does His best work in the dark. When God hides you, remember that He's preparing you, for where He intends on taking you. Trust Him, even when you can't trace Him. God was working on you, behind closed doors all along. He was working on you, when they abused you. He was working on you, when they left you. He was working on you, when they talked about you and hated on you. God was working on you then, but He's getting ready to reveal you to the world now. It's your time, to shine in dark times. This is the day, that God is pulling you out of the dark room. You're coming out of the cave to shine, with power from on high.

The path to purpose isn't always smooth. The road to success, goes through some dark places and valleys. It goes through the valley of the shadow of death. The valley is not really substantive, it's just a shadow. God can still arrange for your darkest hour, to mark the dawn of your new day.

FROM SCAR TO STAR

Dr. King declared, "Only when it is darkest, can you see the stars." God has made you a star to shine for Him, because of the trial that He brought you through. For every scar, you will shine like the star you are. For every wound, something wonderful is about to happen in your life. We often train up children, by championing them and telling them to reach for the stars, without acknowledging the darkness that surrounds them. The darkness and difficulty is all necessary, in order to glow in gloomy times.

There are too many people who would rather have their name in lights, than roll up their sleeves and pull somebody out of the dark. They want to be a star, but they don't want to get their hands scarred. A lot of people want the light, but can't handle the heat of hardship. The light is not inseparable from the heat. The light will shine on your scars and struggles too. However, when you have been developed in dark times, you can shine in the good times. The light in you, will bring you through the darkness that surrounds you. When you have eyes of faith, you can see the bright side in a dark moment. God has called you out of darkness, into His marvelous light to do a marvelous work.

UNCOMMON

Somebody in your life, will need an encouraging word from time to time. Let them know like the rapper Common, in an uncommon way, "There are times, when you'll need someone and I will be by your side. There is a light that shines, special for you and me." When you have uncommon faith, then uncommon blessings and breakthroughs happen. Shine your light in an uncommon way, as we live in uncommon times.

GUIDING LIGHT

Don't crash into your past. Stay in your lane and run your race. Stop competing with others and start focusing on your gifts. The only competition is you versus you. Nobody can beat you being you. Beat your best. When you know your purpose and calling, you don't have to answer your critics. The right people will shine with you. Know your worth and let your value shine through. A city set on a hill cannot be hidden. A candle ignited by a flame is meant to shine. In a world of darkness, allow God's Word to be your guiding light. You were created to be great and walk in the uniqueness of your destiny and royalty, purposefully.

HEADLIGHTS

On the road to greatness, stay in your lane and work productively in order to live successfully. You can't drive in a dark world and arrive to your destination, without turning on the headlights. God's glow in you, provides direction and revelation through every situation. Use the light from your eyes of faith. Use the hope in your head, to make sound decisions. Watch the signs God gives you and avoid detours to destruction, on the road to destiny.

FLAWLESS

In Beyonce's song *Flawless,* the Nigerian author Chimamanda Ngozi Adichie speaks on the plight and promise of a girl's transition into womanhood. She says, "We teach girls to shrink themselves, to make themselves smaller. We say to girls: You can have ambition, but not too much. You should aim to be successful, but not too successful. Otherwise, you will threaten the man."

Understand, a real man is not threatened by your ambition, vision, and direction. A grown boy is intimidated but a grown man with a plan, is inspired. Remember, anybody who is intimidated, will always be eliminated. Don't shrink yourself to make others feel big. A real man doesn't mind you shining, whether you're with him on stage, or if he's behind the scenes. He will cheer you on and champion your achievements.

Adichie goes on to say, "We raise girls to see each other as competitors. Not for jobs or for accomplishments, but for the attention of men." When you're too unique to compete, you don't have to vie for the attention of a man.

Real women don't compete they collaborate. They are their sister's keeper. Remember you never have to chase, what you were chosen to receive. What is for you, will happen for you. It can't replace you. Stay in place and position yourself for the best.

Remove yourself from the people that broke you, to make room for the ones who will bless you. Take the light off your flaws and shine it on your faith. Yes, you have made mistakes, but your mistakes don't define you. Focus on your focus. Stop focusing on finding flaws within. You're flawless and you woke up like this. Love yourself. Your potential is limitless. You're flawless, just the way God made you to be!

PETTY OR PRETTY?

Beyonce sang about the pain of being pretty. She said, "Pretty hurts, we shine the light on whatever's worst. Trying to fix something, but you can't fix what you can't see. It's the soul that needs the surgery." You can't glow, by continually shining the light on your weaknesses and flaws.

Your strengths have made you sagacious and flawless. You're special, bright, and beautiful just the way you are. You don't have to compromise or compare yourself, to the women on a TV screen or in a magazine. Why allow 2% of the women who are photoshopped and airbrushed, to control the way you view and feel about yourself? You don't have to be a size 2, to love you! Love the skin you're in. Don't get sucked into a false sense of reality TV. Define your personal reality. Yes, they may talk about you, but let God's love and light shine through you.

Let folks be petty, you just keep being pretty. A pretty woman, knows how to rise above an ugly situation. Yes, pretty hurts, but beauty is coming through your brokenness. Don't dim your light for anybody or anything. Stop reducing yourself, to fit in with people who don't like you anyway.

You weren't born to fit in. You were created to stand out. Stand out and be outstanding. Don't stop shining or lower your value, by settling and getting less than you deserve. Shine on your own and the right person will shine with you. Stop trying to fix on the outside, what God is making over on the inside. Allow Him to heal you from within, so you can shine flawlessly and be pretty!

FLASHLIGHT FAITH

Your phone has a flashlight button to press and shine, to illuminate what is dark. Your life is also like a flashlight, to shine in the face of fear. Flash your light in the face of the enemy. Flash your light in the face of sickness. Let your life be a flashlight, that shines in good and bad times. You may be stuck in the dark, but use the flashlight of faith in God's Word to walk in the light.

GLOW STICK

When I was a little kid, I remember going to birthday parties. The chaperone would pass out a glow stick, to all of the children. Some of the kids, waved the glow stick in the air like they really cared. Some kids, put it around their neck and others would wrap it around their wrist.

In retrospect, one thing I recognized is that the glow stick couldn't shine, until it was broken. Realize, once you've been broken, that's when your anointing and gifts can flow. Your power within, can transform adversity into opportunity and every trial into something triumphant.

The breaking was a setup for a blessing. They thought it was over when they broke you, but it only released the blessing God has for you. I know they dropped you, but you're getting ready to rise again. You may be limping, but a leap is about to lift your spirit.

The only way that the glow stick could shine, was by

being broken. The reason you can shine today, is because you were broken. Your heart was broken. Your marriage was broken. Your community, your home, and your family was broken. They thought that breaking you, would put out your light. However, the breaking only made you shine bright!

Initially, my glow stick couldn't shine, until it was broken. Secondly, my glow stick couldn't shine until all of the lights were out. The problem is, you're trying to shine with lights. You think you're shining, when you get a platform or a photo opportunity with a celebrity. You're trying to shine when the lights come on. Yet I'm wondering, can you shine in the dark?

Can you shine, when nobody will give you an encouraging word? Can you shine, when tears are rolling down your face? Can you shine, when sickness is in your body? Can you shine in the times, when your back is against the wall? Through disappointment, abandonment, failure,

hurt and pain, can you still shine?

The brokenness and the darkness in your life, is all

being used for a greater purpose to make you shine. It's all

working for your good, to position you, to shine in dark

times. Embrace the place of adversity and walk in the

blessing of greater opportunity.

IT'S TIME TO SHINE

Too many people are trying to shine, in a room full of lights.

You need to leave the room and go into some dark places.

Leave your home and go help a sister in a women's shelter.

Don't just tell them about the light of Christ, let them see

Him in you. Everybody gets their time to shine and moment

to own it. This is your prime time. Don't miss your

moment. Don't miss your opportunity to be a blessing.

Shine until depression transforms into joy. Shine until

sickness turns into healing. Shine until sadness becomes gladness.

Go into the communities that are dark and bring light. Go into the hospital room and bring a light of healing. Go into the school and shine. Go, glow, and help somebody to grow. Shine your light in your city. Shine and make an impact. Shine your light in dark communities. Shine and bring unity. Shine your light as a leader. Shine as an innovator and trailblazer. Shine at your job. Shine in your school. Shine with your spouse. Shine in and out of your house. Shine as a family. Shine as a woman of God. Shine as a daughter of destiny. Shine as a lady of liberty. Shine as a queen of quality. This BIG light of mine, I'm going to let it shine! This is your opportunity to shine in a dark world. Let the light in you shine through, when things are dark and dismal around you. It's your time to glow up, grow up, and shine bright!

CHAPTER 7

Strength of a Woman

*Only a strong woman, can go through
and not look like what she's been through.*

T he Queen of Hip Hop Soul, Mary J. Blige in her

song, *Strength of a Woman*, expresses a woman's essence is

found in her selflessness as a giver. In the song, Blige

bellows, "We're the wisdom like a guiding light. We're

the trees left standing through the storms of life." The

darkness around you, could never replace God's guiding light

of love within you. When the storms of life tried to knock

you down, you remained steadfast and kept standing.

I'm sure that you've heard the popular saying, "What

doesn't kill you, makes you stronger." I like to say, "If it doesn't kill you, then use it to build you." Oftentimes, the greatest moments of strength, occur at our weakest moments of hopelessness and despair. It's true that we don't realize how strong we are, until being strong is our only option.

STRONGER

There is strength within you, that you haven't used yet. The obstacles you go through, position you to reveal the strength within you. You have power, that you haven't used yet. Oftentimes, situations in life propel us to exercise strength, that we did not realize we had all along. The power and strength that you have on the inside, will empower you beyond what you're facing on the outside.

Everybody in this life, will face challenges and endure struggles. On the contrary, it's not only about what you go through, it's how you handle what you go through. Life is experienced at a greater level when you can grow through, what was designed to destroy you. The strength of a woman

is not about you possess on the outside. It's about who you

were created to be on the inside. Your strength is forged and

solidified, through the situations that you face!

A MOTHER'S LOVE

As I think about a woman's strength, I pause to reflect on the

strength and love that my mother has exemplified in my life,

for all of my life. She showed me what love is and does, by

the example she set for me and my brother. She continues to

be a source of wisdom and strength, each day. I can reflect

on how strong she was, as a single parent, raising two kids.

Mom taught me how to kick a football, change the oil,

and do what my father should have done. She taught me how

to treat her. She showed me what a gentleman does, in order

to respect and treat a queen. If a man won't treat his mother

right, he sure won't treat you right either. During the most

challenging time of my life, she was right there. I was a kid, who was diagnosed with cancer. Not one day did she doubt, that I could overcome. I've never seen love and strength exemplified, in such a difficult time, during my worst of times. Even when I wanted to give up on myself, mom didn't give up on me.

During my frustrating times, as I was crying and complaining, mama was continually praying. She put the Word of God so deep in me, that sickness and disease had to take their hands off me. I would not be as strong, driven, determined, and ambitious as I am today without my mother's love, strength, and leadership.

She has been a devoted mother, educator of thirty years, earned her Ph.D., author, evangelist, missionary to Jamaica, prayer warrior, encourager, and yes even a disciplinarian when I needed it most. Yes, mama didn't take no mess. She wanted me to be the best. Her strength was immersed in love. She exudes substance, sophistication, style, sagacity, and strength. My mother personifies, the enduring strength of a woman.

Proverbs 31:28 was right when it expressed, "Her children arise and call her blessed." She is immensely blessed, because she has been a blessing to me in so many ways. Only a mother, can give you everything with nothing. If you're a single parent mother, don't give up on your children. Despite how you feel and what they have done. I'm the product of a single parent mother, who didn't give up on me. Keep loving, praying, and being strong for your children in times of weakness.

HOW TO LOVE A STRONG WOMAN

For the woman reading this book, maybe you've had to be strong all of your life. Was there love exemplified in your home? Did you feel loved growing up? Our childhood experiences, have a great impact on our adulthood decisions. So often, we search for what we are void of within. Now we go through life, with all these needs for attention and validation, because no one affirmed us.

Know that your femininity, provides a remedy for the malady of life. Who you are uniquely created to be, is more than the container on the outside. It's about your content on the inside. The content of your character, is more important than what's on your outer container. Does your heart and mind contain love? The tragedy is to have a heart, but not have a heart. It's meaningless, if it's loveless.

Your cute eyes mean nothing, if they don't have a vision. Your pretty hands are useless, if you won't stir up your gift and help somebody. There is a hidden treasure, within the recesses of your womanhood and femininity. A lot of times, people who have been hurt develop defense mechanisms. When your expectation and experience don't align, it produces pain all the time. When you've been hurt for years, you become tough and callous. When you have learned how to survive on your own, you build up a level of resistance. You cope internally and decide, that you will be strong for you. As a result, you conceptually built a Great Wall of China and a Berlin Wall of emotions, because you had to protect your heart. Maybe you find yourself saying things like, "I don't need a man." You tell your girlfriends, "What can a man do for me?" Well, the right one can do, what the wrong one was never capable of doing.

Due to hurt, you begin to harden your heart and even reject what you're most desiring of, that being love. Can anyone blame you for your disposition? Look at what you've survived through and overcome? Think about it. You were the one, who had to take the car to the auto shop and fight with the mechanic yourself. You were the breadwinner, working multiple jobs while raising multiple children. You took out the trash and cut the lawn. You lifted the heavy furniture, that a man with sculpted biceps and triceps, didn't try to do. You were the one, who put your heart on your sleeve and got it broken. You cooked dinner for the kids, tucked them in at night, took them to school, picked them up, and brought them home. You provided for everybody, when no one provided for you. All that you do and have been through, embodies the strong woman that you grew into. All the hats you wear and all the pressure that's on you.

I applaud you. Who can blame you? You had to wipe your own tears. You had to encourage and counsel yourself. You had to put on makeup and smile on the outside, when you were hurting on the inside. Only a strong woman like you, can go through and not look like what she's been through. You've had to be strong for yourself, when no one was strong for you. A weak man, can't love a strong woman like you.

What happens when you're tired of being strong? It tears at the core of who you are. No weak person can understand the strength, you exercise each day. You understand, it's not easy being a woman. It's not easy going through, what you have been through. Yet God still strengthens you. In times of weakness, He is your strength.

Only a strong man can love a strong woman, who deals with situations that can weaken the spirit. A strong man will pick you up, where you are and position you where you need to be. A strong man will strengthen you, when you're struggling. He's strong enough to know, that it's not about loving a thousand women. It's about loving one special woman, a thousand ways that matters most. A man of character is caring, committed, compassionate, and creative. He ensures that your strong connection is rooted in Christ. On behalf of good brothers like me, we recognize and salute your strength, through stress and times of struggle.

BATTLE, BROKENNESS, BREAKTHROUGH

Maybe you have a good man. However, you find yourself wrestling with the one you have now, because you didn't get over the one you had then. You're in a battle, accusing and blaming him, because you're preoccupied with what the last man didn't do. How can you be virtuous, if you're vicious? If you're argumentative, fighting, nagging, and disrespecting him, then you will lose a good man in the process. You will always get more out of a man, if you encourage him. Rather than, complain to him and about him. Yes, he loves you and he's good to you. However, he will not continue to be treated bad by you. If you want a gentleman, you must be a gentlewoman. Be the woman who is gentle, genuine, courteous, kind, and empowers him through the genius in your mind.

Could it be, that the festering anger you project on others, is due to what you didn't disconnect from in your past? No relationship will grow, until you let go. Let the baggage battle go. Let go of the defense mechanism and heal from the past, so you can walk jointly into your future. If you adjust your attitude, then your altitude will cause you to aspire higher.

Everything doesn't always go as planned. Your children may not have turned out, the way you planned for them to be. Even the relationship didn't have the ending, that you envisioned in your mind. Be encouraged in knowing, you can still have victory even in the face of impending calamity.

Heal from what hurt you, so you can love who loves you. The battle that you're in, is yours to win. For the battle is not yours, but it belongs to the Lord. Let Him be your shield and buckler, to break you through what was intended to break you. Let God bring you through the battle of brokenness, into a place of blessings and breakthrough.

YOU OWE IT TO YOU

The Jamaican Reggae artist Shaggy, conveys the strength of a woman, in his lyrics from the song *Strength of a Woman.* He says, "Tender lips that's so sweet. Gentle words she softly speaks. Such an angel when we need. God bless the ground beneath her feet. She can take you on a high. Be your comfort when you cry. If you look into her eyes, you'll see the strength of a woman."

The wise words that flow, from the lips of a woman of strength are indeed a precious jewel. Your nurturing nature and gentle femininity, are just a few of the attributes that make you uniquely special. Even a blind man can recognize your strength, that goes beyond what the eyes can see. Only a heart of love can reveal, what sight is limited to perceive.

There is greater strength, hope, and healing that resides in your heart. You know you're healed, when you can look in the mirror and tell yourself how beautiful you look, without craving validation from someone else. You're healed, when you can take yourself to dinner, by yourself. You're healed, when you can send yourself flowers and be just as excited, as if someone gave them to you. If you don't like yourself and mistreat yourself, you will mistreat someone else. Be good to yourself.

Don't get upset about where you've been. Get excited about where you're going. Other women didn't make it through, what you've been through and you're still here. Look at the trials you've been through and overcome. Count your blessings. You made it! You better be good to yourself. Don't expect anybody else to appreciate you, if you don't appreciate you. Cheer yourself on! You owe it to you. If nobody celebrates you, celebrate the strength of a woman in you!

CHAPTER 8

Leading Lady

*If you don't know who you are,
you can't lead anybody anywhere.*

As a *WOMAN* you **W**onderfully **O**rchestrate **M**agnanimous **A**chievements **N**aturally. As a leading lady who wears many hats, you give life and speak life, into those who desire to get more out of life. More than ever before, women like you are changing the world at a rapid rate.

We are seeing women lead, in almost every facet of life. Women are branding, starting businesses and building their queendom. Leading ladies are entrepreneurs, nurses, doctors, lawyers, judges, teachers, principals, politicians, beauticians, domestic engineers, and all around trailblazers.

You can't deny the power that women have, especially in a society that is ever-changing. Yet the more things change, the more they seemingly stay the same.

Madeleine Albright, the first woman to become U.S. Secretary of State expressed, "There is plenty of room in the world for mediocre men, but there is no room for mediocre women." Since your childhood, you have always been held to a higher standard. Your brother got away with things, you couldn't do. Double standards have pervaded through your life, all of your life. Men can seemingly violate societal standards, that a woman could never violate.

WHAT IS ENOUGH?

We see this time and time again, when men who don't have the pedigree, education, or skill set required are hired. They are paid more than women, who are more qualified and can do a better job. Race, class, and gender are always pertinent issues that we grapple with daily. As a woman you're held to a higher standard, especially for employment. Your hair has to be done a certain way. Your dress has to be long enough. Your diction has to be clear enough. Sometimes your skin has to be "light enough" and even still that's not good enough. Now you find yourself asking, "What is enough?"

However, a man can throw on a jogging suit and get that same job, you applied for, when he's not even qualified to have it. Oftentimes, if the application is marked "female" some employers have a "we'll think about it" gender inequity philosophy. These are issues that build walls, instead of bridges and ladders for leading ladies. Sadly, the ideals of inequality and the culture of chauvinism, shoves leading ladies out of the door of opportunity.

Albeit, I find it interesting that Mrs. Albright mentioned that women, not men were the ones who made her feel inadequate. The insecurities, stereotypical and negative ideals that pervaded in their own minds, were used to punch at the vision in Mrs. Albright's life. Briefly, let's subtract men from the equation. How many times have you been put down by another woman, because of her own insecurity and jealousy? She tries to stop you from upward mobility, because she doesn't have the courage to be all that she can be.

When you are your sister's keeper, you don't compete but you collaborate. People who live in doubt, will try to diminish your dreams and turn it into a nightmare. Shake off feelings of inadequacy, because you are enough. In fact, God has given you more than enough, to move forward. See when you're blessed, you can do more with less.

BREAK THE GLASS CEILING

Yes, you may be the only woman in the room, but speak up. Don't retreat to satisfy and soothe the opinions of others.

They're going to say, "Who does she think she is anyway?" Let them know, by the wisdom that flows from you. You're in the boardroom, at the hospital, in the classroom, and at the executive board meeting because you have something to say. Your ideas matter, so don't be afraid to convey them. Your idea and ingenuity, can save a company. It can address a population of people, who are underserved because of your perspective.

Don't be afraid to use your hammer of hope, to break barriers and glass ceilings, that seek to trap women like you. The aspect of a glass ceiling, paints the image that you can look up and see through it, but you can never get to what you're looking through. Have I lost you? You can see it, but you can't attain it. You can see greatness, but you can't grab it. Oftentimes, what prevents you from breaking through, to the other side, is the fear and insecurity you grapple with on the inside.

How many times, has life been like a mirage for you? When you see it and would stretch out to get it, you couldn't find it. What you thought was there, had either left or was never there in the first place.

The marriage was a mirage. The man was a myth, because he wasn't who you thought he was, or who he said he was when you initially met him. The car, the home, the kids, the job, and the career all seems to disappear. Have you ever found yourself in a place, where it seems like everything good to you and for you, alludes you?

All the blessings seem to pass over you, to somebody else. Everybody is getting married but you. Co-workers are getting promoted except you. The lady across the street, just got a new car and you're still driving a wonder car. You continue to "wonder" is the car going to get you, from point a to point b. Stop focusing on what you don't have and begin to praise God, for what you do have. He has more wonderful blessings, in store for you. Just because it hasn't happened yet, doesn't mean it won't come to pass. It's not delayed or denied. When it's time, it will happen at the right time. Don't get trapped in a feeling, break the glass ceiling!

LEADING WHILE BLEEDING

So often, we find ourselves helping others the most, when we're hurting the most. When you're in places and positions of leadership, you always have to be "on" by being poised and polished. You know the routine. Smile for the camera, give eye contact, shake hands, and kiss babies. You put on your best face, when you walk in any place. Sometimes you get to a point, where your back is against the wall and you're too weak to be strong. Naturally, you're a helper. Everyone comes to you with problems and you always have an answer. You help your girlfriends, but whose helping you? The advice you give keeps people's marriages together, but yours is falling apart. Who is the strong friend, that checks on you in your time of weakness? Who encourages the encourager? Remember, you are the CEO: Chief Encouraging Officer of your life.

Oftentimes, we become everything to everybody, but nothing to ourselves. As a result, we find ourselves leading while bleeding. Hurting internally, but smiling externally. You put makeup over your mess. You get dressed and put a skirt, over your scars and stress. You put a band-aid over your bruises and promise to never let them see you sweat. You stay busy, because you don't want to deal with the issues that eat away, at your serenity and tranquility. Have you ever worked as hard, as you've hurt? The pain and perspiration, makes it hard to distinguish, between the sweat that flows down your face and the tears that fall from your eyes.

Isn't it interesting that you can be dressed up, smelling good, makeup perfect, hair done, nails flawless, and still feel ugly internally? All the while, other people are jealous of you but don't have a clue that under that designer dress, heels, and jewelry you're harboring pain, resentment, anger, hurt, and insecurity. You smile through the sadness, while you silently scream and writhe in pain. On one side, you're leading, working, and fighting off the haters. On the other side, you're trying to heal from the horrific hemorrhaging hardship, wounds, and scars.

People will erroneously judge you, but don't have a clue about what you've been through. Let them roll their eyes, smack their lips, and talk about you behind your back. God will use it all, to bless you in front of their face. When they doubt you, God will promote you. God is about to show your critics, that His Word is stronger than their words. While they're laughing at you, God is blessing you. Yes, you've gone through, but you don't look like what you've been through. In adversity, God sustained you through it all, to not only survive but thrive. He has a blessing to heal and mend, the angst and aching in your soul. You will not suffer, but you will recover. The scar will become your greatest strength. The suffering will lead to your biggest blessing. You are gifted despite being afflicted. Even now, God is strengthening you as a leader, to do your greatest ministry in the midst of great misery.

BEING VS. DOING

If I was talking to a group of leading ladies and asked the question, "Who are you?" most women would begin to tell me what they do. Many would say, "I'm a nurse, stay at home mom, clinical technician, engineer, lawyer, business owner, etc." I didn't ask what you do, I asked who are you. What you do is surface, but who you are is substance. Doing is about performing, but being is about positioning. How are you positioning your life? Not for a career, fame, fortune, or a man but for yourself. How can you be good to anybody else, if you're not good to yourself first? Too often we focus on doing something, that we disregard being somebody. Start being what you always wanted to be, by identifying who you are and being good to yourself in the process. What is your identity? You will never know who you are, until you know whose you are. Who are you, outside of what you possess or the title in front of your name?

Doing the role of a mother or wife, is different than being a mother or wife. You can be connected to it and operate in the role of it, but be totally disconnected from it. If there is no love, compassion, mindfulness, and heart, then things will fall apart. Stop trying to be, what you already are. You're already powerful. Already beautiful. Already wonderful. Already successful. Already a leading lady. Just be it, so you can do whatever it is that you desire to do. Daniel 11:32 declares, "For the people that know their God,

WOMAN - DR. EDDIE CONNOR

shall BE strong and DO exploits." Don't just keep doing, start

being and things will begin working in your favor. If you just

become it, you won't have to chase it. What you need and

want will chase you!

SPEAK LIFE

If you keep focusing on what you haven't received, you

never will receive it. Change what you're thinking. Change

what you're speaking and you will change what you're

getting. Start speaking life to your situation. You're thinking,

"Well nothing is happening. I'm not getting anything." The

reason you aren't getting anything, is because you haven't

said anything. Open your mouth and speak life, to dead and

dry places! Live through dying places. Begin to break

through, what was designed to break you. If you believe,

then you will begin to win before the race begins.

This is the season and this is the year, that everything

that was over your head, is now going to be under your feet. Break the ceiling of sadness, to experience joy. Break the glass of your past, to walk into your future. The next generation, is dependent upon what you do now. You were created to blaze a trail, that can prevail against every hater and naysayer.

LEADERS WHO DON'T LOVE

A lot of times, people deem the title of leader, as something reserved for men only. Leadership is not about masculinity or femininity, it's about personal identity. If you don't know who you are, you can't lead anybody anywhere. Leadership is not power driven, it's servant driven. The great ones know how to serve others. Serving is your path to succeeding. Leadership is not selfish, it's selfless. In a "friend me" and "follow me" social media generation, real leadership is not about how many followers you have on your page. Real leadership is about how many leaders you create, from those who follow you. Real leaders empower followers, to turn the page and write a new chapter.

Dr. Cornel West poignantly suggests, "You can't save the people, if you won't serve the people. You can't lead them, if you don't love them." Who do you turn to, when the people that should nurture and love you, now turn on you or away from you? Sadly, these are the sentiments from many of our girls and women.

There are too many leaders, whether male or female, who are void of love. They have the title of leader, but lack the essence of a leader. They have the leadership position, but lack the love and discipline, to function in the position. Nothing is worse, than leaders who don't love. Leaders who are in the position as head, but lack heart. They don't care for the least, the lost, the last, and the littlest among us. Their narcissism, pathology, and greedy mentality will drive them, to take from those who don't have, to have more themselves.

As a result, our brothers and sisters are regarded as societal outcasts and throwaways. They are overlooked, underserved, and underrepresented. They are unloved, not only by the larger society, but oftentimes in their own community. We see too many forces, preying on the lives of our brothers and sisters, rather than praying for the lives of our brothers and sisters. A sickening psychosis makes the powers that be, more desirous of locking them in prison, rather than unlocking their potential.

SERVANT LEADERSHIP

The essence of leadership hinges, on what you're willing to let go of to gain. You can't lead, if you don't love. You can't build and save, if you won't bless and serve. So many times we see life, as a highlight reel or a reality show and become blinded by the lights. Leadership is not what takes place in the lights, the fundamental form of it is forged through character in the dark. People will open their eyes to admire the fruits of your labor, but close a blind eye to the seeds you sowed to reap the harvest.

You are the Superwoman that we have been looking for, time and time again. However, the "S" on your chest, doesn't always stand for Superwoman, success, or strength. Sometimes the "S" on your chest, symbolizes that you're sad, sensitive, and struggling. The pain that you endured, can help someone else whose dealing with it like you.

As a leading lady, you are a servant leader, who can forge something great in our homes and communities. The essence of servant leadership, goes beyond a title and seeks to commit your time. Servant leadership is more concerned about reconciliation, than recognition. This type of leadership, is ingrained in devotion to a worthy cause.

Dr. King declared, "Everybody can be great, because anybody can serve. You don't have to have a

WOMAN - DR. EDDIE CONNOR

college degree to serve. You don't have to make your subject and verb agree to serve. You only need a heart full of grace. A soul generated by love." A heart of grace, a soul of love, and a mind to serve, is what will transform girls into women of destiny, who manifest their purpose in the community. Simply because, the greatest leader is a servant leader.

The concept of "servant leadership" was coined by Robert K. Greenleaf. In his essay, *The Servant As Leader* he wrote, "The servant-leader is servant first. It begins with the natural feeling that one wants to serve. Then conscious choice brings one to aspire to lead." Greenleaf goes on to suggest, "The servant makes sure that other people's highest priority needs, are being served. The best test, and difficult to administer, is: Do those served grow as persons? Do they, become healthier, wiser, freer, more autonomous, more likely themselves to become servants?

And, what is the effect on the least privileged in society? Will they benefit, or at least not be further deprived?"

The power of serving and leading, has to be a calling. It can't be about notoriety, it has to be driven by one's nobility of dignity and character. It's not about receiving applause. It's about rolling up your sleeves, to work, for a purpose and cause.

Formal education, accolades, success, money, and attaining more degrees than a thermometer, is not the litmus test of leadership. The substantive framework, is via the foundation of servitude. The life and ministry of Jesus, provides the greatest example of servant leadership. In Matthew 23:11, Jesus declared, "He that is greatest among you, shall be your servant."

LEADING LEGACY

The structure of servant leadership, is about making the objectives clear and rolling up your sleeves, to help others succeed. In that vein, they don't work for you, but you work for them. Leadership is more than a title or a position, it's a function. Since it is a function, you must take action.

Real leadership causes you to be self-reflective. The question is: Are you here to do something, or are you here just for something to do? If you're on this planet to do something, then what is it? What difference will you make? What will be your legacy? What is your passion? What is it that energizes you? Other than your alarm clock, what wakes you up in the morning? How driven are you to succeed? Do you want to be good or great? Average or amazing? Ordinary or extraordinary? What will you do, to improve the lives of other people?

Possessing passion is not enough, you must transform your passion into action. What you dedicate yourself to, has to consume you each day. You must find the motivation and inspiration within. It must be authentic. You can't be lackadaisical and lazy. Nothing worth working for is easy, that's why it's called hard work.

Life is not social media. It's not about how many people "like" you. It's really about how much love, you have for yourself and others. You can't reflect love, if you don't possess love within. Real leadership isn't measured by the number of followers, that someone has on Facebook, Instagram, Twitter, and Snapchat. Real leadership is about the number of leaders, that one creates. True leadership must be for the benefit of the followers, not to just enrich the leader. How will you create and cultivate, a leading legacy?

PERFORMANCE OVER POPULARITY

As a leading lady, understand that leadership is not about popularity, it's about performance. When you're committed to the task at hand, you will be committed to be the best that you can be. Begin to tap into the untapped potential and power within you. Realize that what you own on the outside, pales in comparison to the richness on the inside of you.

THE RELATIONSHIP OF LEADERSHIP

There can be no real leadership, without developing healthy relationships. Real leaders are not dictatorial, they are relational. They build caring and committed relationships, that go beyond *I* and *Me*, to focus on *Us* and *We*. Real leaders operate from a "show and tell" standpoint. They lead by example, to where their actions do the talking. Too many people's lips are moving, but their actions aren't saying anything. They believe in lip service, but not leadership as a service.

There is no true leadership, without personal ownership and sometimes that means saying, "I messed up." Just because you messed up, doesn't mean you have to give up. A knockdown is not a knockout, unless you stay down.

Get back up and get back in the fight. Brush your shoulders

off and learn from your mistakes. In the words of singer

Lionel Richie, "You're once, twice, three times a lady."

Yes, you may be a wife, but you're still a leader in life.

You follow God and your husband, but there are some

leadership qualities that you possess too. You're just not

docile and weak, you have a mind as well.

Do you know how to separate your career and

independent woman ideals, that can produce fissures in

relationships? Do you still have a need to be the boss in your

marriage, just because you're the boss in the marketplace?

Yes, we know a real man is not intimidated, but he does want

to be complemented. How do you use your strengths to

complement weak areas in relationships, ministries, careers,

and with everyday people?

4 TYPES OF LEADING LADIES

1. *Envisioners* see the BIG picture. They are good at thinking outside of the box. They look far into the future and develop creative solutions, to problems or new ways of thinking about them. They often come up with big plans and then pass on those plans to others, to implement.

2. *Analyzers* are orderly, systematic, concrete, and fact-oriented leaders. They like measurable goals, structure, predictability, and they also like tackling problems. Being organized is key and important to them.

3. *Feelers* often wear their heart, on their sleeve. They are open-hearted leaders, for whom building relationships is the highest priority. They are perceptive, intuitive, and completely people-oriented. Feeler-type leaders are empathetic, spontaneous, and often place little value on formality. They are driven emotionally and as a result,

speak unabashedly from a feeling, oriented perspective.

4. **Doers** are leaders who want to get the job done. They are results-oriented and high-energy individuals. They are always on the move. Doers are decisive. Their actions speak louder than words. They are also good at multitasking and juggling many responsibilities at once.

Which type of leader are you? Are you a combination of any two? What abilities, gifts, qualities, and perspectives do you bring to the table that aren't listed? What specific portion listed is not your strong point? How can you use it, as a building block to get better?

STAY ON T.R.A.C.K.

Transparency - Know the truth about who you are, including your strengths and weaknesses. If you don't know who you are, people will tell you what you're not. Be authentic.

Resilience - Bounce back from setbacks. It's a setup for a greater comeback. Remain positive in negative situations. Be persistent and push. Tough times don't last, tough people do.

Attitude - Your attitude determines your altitude. Provide access and opportunity, for the people you serve with a smile.

Character - There are three sides to people: 1. Who you pretend to be, 2. Who people think you are, 3. Who you really are, which is the true essence of character. Talent will take you to the top. Only character, commitment, and compassion will keep you on top.

Kindness - Treat others how you want to be treated. If you desire respect, then give it so you can receive it. Maintain an open ear, open mind, and an open heart to lead with love.

GOLDEN LADY

Stevie Wonder, one of the supreme songwriters and musical geniuses of our generation, masterfully muses about a *Golden Lady*. Stevie's *Innervisions* paints a vivid picture, providing ability beyond his inability to see. Even in being blind since birth, he sings "Looking in your eyes. Kind of heaven eyes." How does Stevie see, what he can't see? You see, sight is of the eyes, but vision is of the mind and heart.

Yes, Stevie lost his sight, but he gained insight. He can see a woman's value despite his blindness. On the contrary, it's rather interesting that some people with good sight, are still blind to your value. They have cataracts, when it comes to your character. Some have selective sight. They can only see your behind, but not the greatness in your mind.

In the song, Stevie goes on and wonderfully expresses "It's so clear to me that you're a dream come true, there's no way that I'll be losing." Simply because, a man understands that to lose a good woman like you, is the utmost loss. The loss is greater than money. You can't put a price on what it will cost you, to lose her value. Golden lady, your ability and stability, empowers a man to win. Essentially, losing you is not worth it, because you're worth more than money can buy or words can express.

Begin to live your life, like it's golden. Continue to think big, follow through on your big ideas, and lead by example as a cultivator and communicator. You're as good as gold. You're more than someone's type. You are the prototype that any good man, would desire to behold and hold. To have a leading lady like you for a lifetime, is too golden of an opportunity to pass over.

CHAPTER 9

Daughter of Destiny

Adversity orchestrates your purpose,
to align with your destiny.

See yourself as a leading lady of liberty. Look at your life in 3D, as a Divine Daughter of Destiny! Adjust your vision, expand your mind, and begin to expect provision. God is your Heavenly Father and you are His daughter of destiny. Any real father, wants his daughter to be the best and have the best. Your Heavenly Father wants you, as His daughter, to be the best and have the best as well. God gave His SON to erase your dark past and bring the SUN into your life, so you can shine for the rest of your life.

He wants His daughter of destiny, to have the best son of substance, that will love and empower you. Before you dwell on the man of your destiny and dreams, keep taking the necessary steps to fulfill your destiny and dreams. In due time, you will merge with the right one on the road to your God ordained destiny.

BIRTH YOUR DESTINY

This ninth chapter is unique, because the number nine symbolizes birthing. If you're a mother, you know that in order to give birth to your baby, you have to push. There is a daughter of destiny inside of you, that has to come forth. Your dream has been locked up and delayed long enough. It's time to birth your destiny and deliver your dream. Whatever you do, keep pushing. Push through the storm. Push through the rain. Push through heartache and pain. Push through the haters and naysayers. Push through abuse. Push forward and give birth to the reality of your dreams!

It's time to deliver and push out your dream. You've

been talking about starting the business, but you still haven't mapped out the plan. You keep saying that you're going to write the book. However, you can't finish until you start. How long will you keep telling yourself, that you're going back to school to get your degree? This is your year to enroll.

Stop talking and start creating. Start working and begin pushing out the vision that's in you. You will continue to be frustrated and unfulfilled, until it's revealed. Push out your destiny and purpose, because you're pregnant with potential. Don't let it die inside of you. If you put in the labor, then God will release His favor.

Everything you need is ready to be birthed, but you have to push. You will remain uncomfortable, until you manifest the entrepreneurial gift inside of you. Don't abort your vision. Don't let your destiny die. Don't allow negativity to take up residence in your mind. Give birth to your goals and dreams. Push out your dream and destiny. Don't let anything cripple you or stop you. PUSH! After you *Pray Until Something Happens*, then begin to *Praise Until Something Happens*! Whatever you do, PUSH!

GET READY AND STAY READY

Getting married won't heal you and being single won't kill you. Be content, in whatever state you are in. Wait on God or the weight of rushing, will hurt you in the long run. It's better to wait for the right one, than settle for just anyone right now. Being alone doesn't mean you're lonely. It just means you're getting ready.

What you're getting ready to gain, is better than what you lost. Don't lose your mind over the person in your past, because you're going to need your mind for the one that's coming. Trust and believe that what is ahead, is far greater than what you left behind. The dream you're about to receive, is greater than the nightmare you released.

Stop holding on to people, who have let you go. Start letting go of negative people, who are holding on to you. Negative people will only hold you back, from your destiny and purpose. Don't abort your vision, your future, or your destiny. Deliver and birth it. Cancel your subscription, to every negative issue. It's over, let it go. You can't change the past, but you can presently shape your future. You have love under new management. As a daughter of destiny, take control of your life, get in the driver's seat, and press forward on the road to your destiny. Your destiny awaits because power, promise, purpose, and possibility is on the other side of pain.

IT AIN'T FOR EVERYBODY

You can't take everybody with you, on your journey to destiny. If I was driving a *Ferrari Pininfarina Sergio*, why would I try to cram ten people into it? The vehicle was only made for two people. It just won't work. Stop trying to make a relationship work, that God didn't design to fit your destiny. Stop trying to fit people, where they don't belong.

The same concept applies to life. You can't take everybody with you. Everybody can't go, where God is taking you. It's not personal, it's just based on principle. Your purpose, is more important than pleasing people. If God is pleased with you, it doesn't matter if people aren't. Don't try to fit people from your past or present, into your future. Make the adjustments and you will save yourself, the headache and heartache.

ASSETS ONLY

People are portals, who either bring what is positive or negative into your life. As assets or liabilities, they will either add to your value or subtract from it. If they are not adding, then subtract them from your life. Decide to surround yourself with assets only, because liabilities will make you feel lonely. God only brings people into your life, to add and multiply. If people bring division in your life, to divide you from your destiny and subtract your substance, then it's time to do some personal inventory. Recognize the signs. Stop spending time with what God didn't send. Unnecessary relationships, will take you through unnecessary changes. You can't change someone, if God didn't change them first.

When you really know your worth, you will surround yourself with people who enhance it, not diminish it. Your value doesn't diminish, because someone failed to recognize it. Don't lose your value, because someone lost sight of who you are. As a daughter of destiny, don't beg someone to see what they weren't given eyes to recognize. Yes, it may hurt, but just know that adversity is only a setup, to align you with your destiny.

DOORS OF DESTINY

Some people were only meant to be a part of your history, but not your destiny. Stop recycling, what God is replacing. Start preparing for the one, that God is preparing for you. This time it won't be a mismatch, but your destiny will make the perfect match. Shut the door on relationships that have kept you discombobulated, depressed, and defeated. I know it's simple to say, but it takes courage to do it. Break the cycle of bad habits, toxic relationships, stinking thinking, and low level living. Your gifts are the keys, to break out of the old and unlock the new doors of destiny.

TOY STORY

It doesn't matter how old you are, you're never too old to be inspired by a children's movie. In the movie *Toy Story*, the character *Buzz Lightyear* reminds us, that we are on the path, "To infinity and beyond." Lay aside everything that weighs you down, so your dark night can manifest into a light year. It's a new dawn and a new day in your life. This is your time to walk in the light of love, healing, hope, and prosperity.

Don't let anybody treat you like a toy. Don't let them play with your emotions, wind up your expectations, twist you in a trap, and treat you like a joker. You're not some toy, that after someone ripped off the wrapping paper and played with the object, now they're bored and don't want it anymore. You're not an object, that somebody can pick up and put back on the shelf. A lot of people who extend their hands, will mishandle you. They didn't come to give, only to take.

Realize that God purchased you with a price and you are priceless. You are not a toy but a treasure, that must be valued. God placed a gift within you. You can't put yourself in everybody's hands, because people will mishandle you. People will drop you, bruise you, and break you without any consolation, remedy, or conscience of their mistreatment.

You will look up and find yourself, trying to recover from

years of pain. You're a gift to somebody and if they

don't recognize it, that's their loss!

Don't let anybody, kill your buzz or become a barrier

to your breakthrough. Just like *Toy Story* suggested, "To

infinity and beyond." You're *beyond* drama, *beyond*

brokenness, *beyond* depression, *beyond* low self-esteem,

beyond abuse, and *beyond* bitterness. Get to the *beyond* stage

of your life, so that you can walk into the bright path of your

destiny and future.

KISS IT GOODBYE

One of the greatest entertainers and musicians to ever live, is

my late cousin Prince. Maybe you know of his popular song

entitled, *Kiss*. One particular lyrical stanza said, "Women not

girls rule my world. Act your age mama, not your shoe size."

Maturity not just femininity, provides a stark difference between a girl and a woman. A girl contains the essence of womanhood, but maturity ushers her into adulthood. As there are men who act like boys, so too there are women who act like girls. The tragedy is when the boy or girl, acts more mature than the adult.

You can't rush something, that has to take its course naturally. Don't rush what God wants you to mature into. Let character take its natural course. Stop rushing the blessing. When it's time, things will work out fine.

Prince closes the song, with these words, "I just want your extra time and your kiss." Too often you've given your extra and precious time to the wrong people. Have you ever given your love to someone, who betrayed you with a kiss? You trusted them and they treated you like trash. God is delivering you from Judas type people, whose lips say one thing, but do another. Judas' betrayal of Jesus was used as a vehicle, to get Christ to the cross. You have to endure the tests and trials to be qualified. You can't skip the steps. Essentially, you can't get a crown without a cross. When you get betrayed and carry your cross, just know there is a crown coming. Your next kiss won't be from a Judas, it will be from a jewel that God will use to lift your life. A Judas will betray you with a sweet kiss, that leaves bitter scars. A jewel shares truth, love, and inspiration that heals scars to make your life better.

However, there comes a time in your life, where you have to say goodbye to something. In order to get the jewel, you have to kiss the junk goodbye. Find the good in goodbye.

Are you going to stay in an abusive and toxic relationship or let it go? Are you going to remain in your old ways or step into new level living? Choose ye this day. What you're familiar with, is choking your dreams. Can you exercise strength, by letting it go and kissing it goodbye? Can you leave limited relationships, with limited people that don't bring about purpose? There are a lot of people around you, who are not with you. They are in your circle, but they're not connected to you. Kiss your past goodbye. Yes you may be fine, but you're not what God had in mind. So long, bye bye.

Tell your old life goodbye. Kiss sickness goodbye. Kiss negative thoughts goodbye. Kiss depression, anger, and loneliness goodbye. Kiss cancer, cysts, crisis, and chaos goodbye. Kiss debt, doubt, and disease of all kinds goodbye. God is your healer, provider, and protector. Kiss poverty and generational curses goodbye. Release it and be restored. Let it go and watch your life grow. In order to move forward into your future, you have to say goodbye to your past.

Better is coming. You can't receive what's better, by holding on to what's bitter. You are a woman of royalty.

There is a queen in you. Begin to walk, talk, act, and live

like it. You are a lady of liberty and a divine daughter of

destiny!

CHAPTER 10

Queen of Quality

A queen of quality is not needy, she's needed.

A queen of quality, is focused on investing in herself and others. She is an asset, not a liability. Yes, a lot of women refer to themselves as "queen" these days. Maybe I'm partly to blame, because I wrote the book. However, what is a queen, if you don't know who you are as a woman? Notice, I didn't refer to what you do. I mentioned who you are. Who are you underneath the makeup, dress, hair, heels, and earrings? If you don't know you, then you leave it to someone to define you.

A queen is not some inanimate object, celebrity figure, lifeless mannequin, or regal title to attain. A queen of quality knows who she is, as a woman. She is the type to chase her purpose and plan, not a man. She isn't so thirsty for love, that anybody can quench it. She knows her value, loves herself, and becomes a magnet for love. She's not the woman that needs a man. She's the woman that a man needs. What necessitates her being needed, is that she's not needy. She has a plan, purpose, and identity. When you have self-awareness and love yourself, then you don't just settle for something and chase anything. You know that God, will give you the best of everything.

If people don't recognize your value, that's their loss. Don't beg anyone to see, what they choose to remain blind to. The right one will see and celebrate your value. Queen, take comfort in knowing, that your king will find you and complement your life. He won't just compliment you with flattering remarks, on your outer appearance. He will complement your inner vision and attributes, as a companion on the road to destiny. Don't look for somebody to complete you, God does that. You will remain incomplete, by looking for people to complete you. Take it out of their hands and put it in God's hands. He has the perfect person for you, that's perfect for you. Embrace who you are. You're the right type, so prepare for your prototype.

QUALITY OVER QUANTITY

On this planet, there are a lot of women but very few are queens. In a world of quantity, be a queen of quality. You can't find a queen of quality on every corner. There are plenty of 7-Eleven convenience stores, but there are far fewer 5 star restaurants. Be a Ruth's Chris in a world of 7-Eleven's. If everyone else is a thrift store, where you can try it on and leave, then be a Saks Fifth Avenue. A queen of quality is not average, she's amazing. You can't find a queen everywhere, because she's rare. A queen is more than a feel good title. It encompasses a life of substance, sagacity, and authenticity.

A queen is more than her assets, she is an asset. Her beauty resides not only on the outside. It shines on the inside. She knows her worth, being priceless from birth. A queen doesn't look for a man to complete her, she knows God does that.

Proverbs 31:19 declares, "She layeth her hands to the spindle, and her hands hold the distaff." A queen is a creator. She doesn't wait for a handout. She puts her hands out and creates something from nothing. She knows that her favor, will yield the fruit of her labor.

Wake up the queen within you. Be the queen, that is driven to make your dream a reality. A queen understands, that her hands will produce her harvest.

NATURAL WOMAN

Aretha Franklin, The Queen of Soul sang, *You Make Me Feel Like A Natural Woman* for a reason. Simply because, when you're natural, you don't have to be artificial or superficial. You don't have to hate, be fake, or phony with other people. You can be genuine, walk in your natural femininity and authenticity. Nobody can beat you, being you. Don't seek the approval of others, by trying to be like them. Stop looking for other people, to make you feel good about yourself. People who don't like or feel good about themselves, will never be able to make you feel good about yourself.

Overcome the opinions of others, so you can hear the true voice within. Walk effortlessly and exude confidence naturally. The most beautiful thing, that any woman can wear is self-confidence. Let the essence of your queen quality, shine effervescently and naturally. Just like the Queen of Soul, be naturally and beautifully you. Let your royalty shine through your smile, soul, and spirit!

NOT NEEDY, NEEDED

You will attract what you are. Become the type of person that you desire to be connected to, because you will attract the type of person that you are within. Your life is a magnet, that will either attract the positive or the negative. You will attract what you're thinking. If your mindset is negative, begin to change your thinking and you will change what you're attracting. You can easily find someone in the club or a vixen, but a virtuous queen is a rare jewel.

Any real man will tell you, there's nothing more attractive than a beautiful, intelligent, sophisticated, goal-oriented, kind hearted, and spiritual woman whose life reflects love. A real man is not only concerned, about the color and curves of a woman. He's impressed by the content of her character. The color that he's most interested in, is comprised of a heart of gold. The curve on your body that's most endearing, is not the form of your hips. It's that smile that adorns your lips. Beyond a woman's curves, a real man understands that your life has endured many curves and winding roads on the path to purpose.

Be the virtuous woman of value, that God created you to be. Never be the type of woman that needs a man, be the type of woman that a man needs. God supplies all of your needs. Let your presence affirm that you're not needy, you're a queen that's needed.

NEVER CHASE, YOU'RE CHOSEN

Queen, you will continually be out of breath and your feet will always be tired, if you're chasing a man. Stop chasing somebody, who doesn't want to be caught. He is alluding and avoiding you, because he's not interested in you. The truth hurts, but it will help you. When you're chosen, you never have to chase. Stop chasing and allow God, to do the choosing. In a world of quantity, know your value, worth, and quality. What is for you, will never run from you. If

you're chosen to receive it, then you won't have to chase it.
Queens don't chase. Queens are pursued by kings. Don't
chase somebody, who is running from you. Any person that
you have to chase, is trying to get away.

INSECURE

The wildly popular show *Insecure,* offers a panoramic
perspective and portrayal, of the modern-day millennial
black woman. It touches deeply on the ups and downs of
relationships, social, and systemic racial issues. *Insecure* is
more than an HBO show, written by Issa Rae. For many,
insecurity is something they struggle with daily. When
you're not happy and secure, you look for things or people
to fill your void within.

When you're not secure in God or yourself, you will
try to place what can't fill the space. Being insecure, will
have you putting people in your rotation, who don't even

deserve to be in position. Insecurity will have you calling

somebody, that you should disconnect from. The nagging

negative of insecurity, will have you hating the reflection

that you see in the mirror. Insecurity will erase your virtue

and purity. Being insecure will have you accusing and

blaming people, for what you do yourself. The inequity of

insecurity, will have you holding on to things that you should

release. When you get real with yourself, then you will begin

to realize the integrity of your destiny, rather than live from a

place of insecurity. Nothing externally can eliminate your

insecurity internally. Get real with you, so you can reveal and

heal what's hurting you.

CELEBRATIONS ARE IN ORDER

Queen, I celebrate you because of the value that you bring.

Nothing on God's green earth, can compare to your value

and self-worth. Realize that you are a person of love and are too unique to compete for love. Never settle or you will get less than you deserve. You are the best and deserve the best. You are precious and priceless. You're too rare to give yourself to just anyone, when God has the perfect one for you.

Be patient. What you want to last, doesn't always happen fast. It's not delayed or denied. It will happen at the right time. While God is preparing you for the right one, He's preparing the right one for you. The right man will cherish, love, and invest in you. For what it's worth, he knows your worth. He will recognize your value, rather than diminish you. A good woman like you is deserving of a good man, who will love, respect, and protect your heart in his hand.

TEAMMATES NOT OPPONENTS

Queen, your king wants to change two things about you: your last name and address. He's impressed by your heart, not just your hips. The most important curve, is the smile that forms on your lips.

This time, the tears that flow down your face will come from the joy of your future, to wash away the pain of the past. The tears will replace, the years of hurt in your heart. Your king will not come to take, but to give greater love to you and reveal the best in you.

The right man knows your worth and will invest in you, to uplift and empower you. The right investment won't leave you emotionally bankrupt, with a broken heart. Be patient and pursue your purpose. God's timing is better than yours. Don't rush it or you will ruin it. While you're trusting and waiting, keep working to invest in yourself. The right one will be an asset, not a liability. You have had enough opponents, start preparing for the right teammate.

A relationship is not a debate team, so why are you arguing? The right one will affirm and appreciate you, not argue with you. The right one will be your teammate, not an opponent. They won't bring pain, they will soothe the pain. A king and queen won't fight each other. They will fight for each other. Real kings and queens, encourage, uplift, support, and pray for each other.

WEAR YOUR CROWN

Wearing a crown doesn't make you a queen, any more than standing in a garage makes you a car. It's the qualities you exude, which qualify you to wear the crown you've been given. Love you, before you expect someone else to.

As you become a person of love, you will become a magnet for love. When your heart is in God's hands, He will give it to the right man who knows how to love, provide, and protect you. Love yourself and know your worth in a greater way, each day. You are worth waiting for and your love is worth looking for. Yes, you've been through crisis, made some mistakes, experienced issues, and dealt with

devastating dilemmas. In spite of it all, there is a queen

inside of you.

People put their feet on you and laughed at you. They

said you weren't gifted or talented, but God has placed a

queen in YOU! Don't let negative thoughts bring you down,

you were created to wear your crown. Lift up your head or

your crown, will fall to the ground. Isaiah 62:3 declares,

"You shall be a crown of glory, in the hand of the Lord."

There is a queen in you, because the King of Kings

gave His life for you. You're a daughter of destiny and a

queen of quality. Just like Kendrick Lamar would say,

"You've got loyalty and royalty inside your DNA." There's

a treasure in you. So wear your crown. Wear your crown of

joy. Crown yourself with greatness. Wear your crown of love.

Wear your crown of righteousness. Wear your crown of

character and creativity. Wear your crown of power and

peace. Don't remove it, wear it boldly! Don't let any clown

take your crown. Wipe your frown and wear your crown,

because there's a queen of quality inside of you!

THE QUEEN CREED

Queens love God.
Queens love themselves and others.
Queens pray.
Queens nurture their children and family.
Queens are strong wives and mothers.
Queens are committed.
Queens display care, character, and compassion.
Queens uplift their community.
Queens bring unity.
Queens recognize the queen in themselves.
Queens strengthen their sisters.
Queens empower their brothers.
Queens respect themselves.
Queens lead and read.
Queens don't compete.
Queens collaborate.
Queens are unique.
Queens have a vision.
Queens are dedicated and educated.
Queens are intellectual and successful.
Queens are their sister's keeper.
Queens wear their crown and build their queendom.

CHAPTER 11

Wonder Woman

Your gender is what makes you female,
but character makes you a woman.

The movie *Wonder Woman*, details the life of an immortal princess, named Diana Prince. She is an adopted daughter of Queen Hippolyta. As she goes into the world, Diana's naiveté makes her completely oblivious, about gender and societal constructs. Due to inequality, she discovers that women are not equal to men.

However, one intangible trait about Diana, is that she is a warrior. She trains to fight and defeat Ares the evil one, in order to bring peace to mankind. It is Diana's love and belief, that empowers her to do a wonderful work. Her femininity enables her, to bring tranquility in a world of disunity.

Just like Diana, you too are an adopted daughter. You're divinely designed with a purpose in mind, as a daughter of the King of Kings. Diana came into the world, but she wasn't of the world. She didn't fit the culture and climate on the planet. She didn't come to the world to start a life, she was there to save lives.

There is more to your life than getting a ring, living in a big house, driving a foreign car, strutting in heels, and holding a fancy handbag. There is a unique call on your life, to bring about change in the world around you. Stop trying to fit, where you don't belong. You were created to excel and do wonders.

WOMAN OF WAR

Diana's life as a warrior, empowered her to defeat the enemy.

Your life as a prayer warrior, will work wonders to defeat every attack the enemy throws at you. When the enemy attacks your body, marriage, relationships, children, and finances, it's time to go to war. You can't just get ready. You have to stay ready. You can't sit idly by and cry or bite your nails. This means war! You have to go into your prayer closet and rebuke the enemy!

Of all the warriors, Diana trained the hardest. I'm glad you pray hard, but I'm wondering how hard are you willing to work for what you prayed to receive? You have to believe that with faith, courage, and God on your side, you can't be denied. You're a wonderful woman, who can work wonders!

Don't let anybody destroy your world. Fight to maintain peace, hope, and joy. Don't let the enemy, steal your serenity and tranquility. Just like *Wonder Woman*, you're being sent into places that are unfamiliar to you. Your gifts are launching you, into unchartered territory. Do something wonderful, that leaves a legacy and empowers your family.

WOMAN'S INTUITION

Your intuition, is for conviction that provides direction. A woman's intuition, is like a key in a car ignition. Its transmission of information, can put you in the right gear to proceed in drive, reverse the direction for protection, or park to wait and avoid red flags. As a woman, you use your intuition, to detect when something isn't right. Your intuition is a spiritual inclination, that navigates you through storms. Recognize the signs, so you don't crash into your past or take a detour to destruction.

Discernment is so key and necessary, in order to decipher between who comes to play and who comes to stay. A real man prepares his life, for his wife. He doesn't intend to rush a woman, knowing that he may ruin it by being in a hurry. He waits on God for direction and guidance.

Essentially, it's better to wait long, than to marry wrong. Pray for discernment, so that God can reveal what has been concealed. His direction is for your protection. The past may have broken your heart, but real love will give you a brand new start. Real love is more than words, its actions will transform your world. The right arms and hands, won't harm or stress you. They will caress and bless you.

Don't be fooled by sleight of hand. Every hand extended is not to give, sometimes it's to take. Stop falling for people, who are not capable of catching you. Make sure they have the right hands to support, love, and strengthen you. Fall in love with someone, who is capable of catching you.

THE "W" ON YOUR CHEST

I'm sure you can confess, the "W" on your chest, doesn't always symbolize *Wonder Woman*, wisdom, or winning.

Sometimes the "W" on your chest, means you're whining, weak, or worried. Many times the struggle is with insecurity, identity, feeling incomplete, addiction, or abandonment. Society has taught us to repress our feelings, rather than express them. So, for years we harbor feelings of anger, resentment, unhappiness, and bitterness all while searching for purpose, and the reality of what it means to be a queen. Living by your emotions and feelings, can wreck your life. Feelings aren't bad, unless they are unchecked and uncontrolled. Don't lose them, just learn how to use them wisely.

FEMALE VS. WOMAN

The definition of a woman, is regarded as "an adult human female." However, I would assert, just like you can be male and not be a man, you can also be female and not be a woman. Just because you have the outer makings, of what a female looks like, that doesn't make you a woman. Gender makes you female, but grandeur and character development qualifies you to be a woman. It takes character to be the woman, that you were created to be. Being a woman is about more than your fingertips, hips, and lips that makes men trip. It's about your character, valor, and virtue that empowers them to stand if they fall. There's nothing like a beautiful woman, with high goals and high standards, in high heels.

Womanhood is about more than your femininity. It's about your identity and mentality, which outweighs your physicality. There is a dichotomy. Gender is what makes you female, but character makes you a woman. It's significant to realize, that you can be a female and still not be a woman. Being born female doesn't make you a woman, any more than standing in a kitchen makes you a chef. It's more than your heels, hips, and manicured hands. It's about your heart. It's more than your body. It's about your maturity. Other than being attractive, what are you attracting? Getting more of this and more of that, will not make you more of a person. More isn't longer or wider. More is deeper. What is your foundation? What are you rooted in?

The fruit of what you harvest, is connected to the root of what you're planted in. Nobody is going to make you feel pretty, if you feel ugly internally. The voice on the outside can't do, what the voice on inside was designed to do. How do you see you? What separates you from the masses beyond your sultry smile, fit frame, or voluptuous physique? More than your femininity, it's about your character, maturity, and personal identity. Being a woman is not about what you possess on the outside. It's about who you were created to be on the inside.

SO YOU CALL YOURSELF A WOMAN?

A real woman understands, that it's not about being knocked

down, that defines her womanhood. It's what she does, after she's knocked down, that defines it. You never lose because you were knocked down. You only lose because you decided to stay down. Even if you have to crawl and cry, get back up and overcome the situation.

To the world you look ordinary, but on the inside you have extraordinary power and potential. Activate your purpose, power, and potential. Brush your shoulders off. Shake yourself and get back in the fight.

You may have been hit, but don't quit. Who are you, beyond what you possess? Who are you, beyond your recognition, notoriety, and success? The essence of your womanhood, has nothing to do with what you have attained. It has everything to do with the power you have gained, as a woman of value and virtue. Remain focused and trust the process. Your blessing will manifest.

PROVERBS 31 WOMAN

Proverbs 31:10 asks, "Who can find a virtuous woman? For her price is far above rubies." In essence, if I can buy her, then she is not the one. It's interesting to note, rubies are found underground. Rubies are literally miles deep, under the ocean floor. A ruby is the most royal, rare, precious, and expensive jewel on the planet. The most expensive ruby to date, sold for an astounding $57.5 million dollars. Yet the Bible affirms, that your value as a virtuous woman, far exceeds that price.

In order to find a ruby, you literally have to dig for it in order to get it. If a man is not willing to search for you and put the work in to get you, then he's not worthy of having you. Your royalty demands loyalty. If he wants you, a gentleman will become a gemologist, in order to find you!

Notice, the scripture never asked, "Who can find a voluptuous vixen?" It doesn't say, "Who can find a pretty face and a slim waist?" Beauty is only skin deep. It's fleeting and it fades. So you won't find that. Rather, you will find a virtuous woman, as the quality of person required. According to Proverbs 12:4, "A virtuous woman is a crown to her husband." She literally upgrades him. A man's life should be better, as a result of being connected to you. A virtuous woman is desirable, unmistakable, and valuable. She operates in modesty, purity, and honesty. In a world of quantity, a woman of quality always stands out because she knows her worth and value.

THE WOMAN AT THE WELL

John chapter 4 highlights the woman at the well, who had five husbands. The current man she was living with, was not her husband. Jesus was talking to her, because he came to restore and give her living water. She was drawing from a physical well, but He wanted her spiritual well to never run dry again.

Much like the woman at the well, what are you thirsting for? See when you thirst for the wrong thing, you end up parched if not dehydrated. Too many people are thirsty for a date, instead of a degree. Thirsty to twerk, rather than to put in the work, to make their dreams a reality. Thirsty for likes on Instagram, but dehydrated when it comes to showing love to the common woman or man. Sometimes you're like the woman at the well, whose back is against the wall. Too often we build a wall, to protect our broken emotions and even see who is worthy enough to break it down.

Underneath your *Superwoman* cape and *Wonder Woman* wardrobe, there is worry. Your cape and wardrobe, becomes a shield to portray your strength and toughness. However, deep in the midnight hour sometimes a little tear, streams down the side of your face and hits the pillow. Nobody knows that you're silently screaming, but you're battling the misery behind the mask. Only God can fill you and heal you of your past. When you're thirsty for God, He will fill you with joy and peace. Nothing can fill the space, that only God can occupy.

WHAT A MAN

Later in that same book (John 4:29), the woman at the well, left her waterpot. She went into the city and said, "Come, see a man who told me everything I ever did." Back in the day, the Hip Hop group Salt-N-Pepa would say, "What a man, what a man, what a man, what a mighty good man."

If a man can speak life, into your life and empower you to grow, then he's a mighty good man. Don't make the mistake of only evaluating him, by the money in his pocket. Seek to draw, from the wealth in his mind and heart.

Don't get caught up in what he drives, find out what drives him. He could have an expensive car, wine you, and dine you. Yet at the same time, drive you into a life of hell,

drama, and abuse. Discover his ambitions and purpose. What

motivates him and what is his vision? Focus on becoming

the right woman and you will get the right man.

HOLLER IF YOU HEAR ME

Recorded in Matthew chapter 15:21-28, is the story of a

Canaanite woman, who had a daughter that was demonically

possessed. She came and fell down at Jesus' feet. According

to customs, they were not supposed to communicate. Jesus

was a Jew and the woman from Canaan, as scholars

suggested, was a black woman. Race has always had an

historical place in our world.

The woman begged Jesus, to cast the demon out of her

daughter. He replied, "It is not right to take the children's

bread, and to cast it to dogs." Maybe you missed that part,

but Jesus referred to the woman as a dog. Most people would

regard that connotation as offensive. I know a few people, who would've given Him a piece of their mind and said, "Jesus you called me what?"

However, as bold as Jesus' statement was, the woman's reply was even bolder. She said, "Truth, Lord: yet the dogs eat of the crumbs, which fall from their masters' table." The woman could have expressed that she was offended, rather she looked past the offense and received her breakthrough. The woman had such a need, that she began to holler. She was too desperate to be denied. When you're at your wit's end and nobody else can do, what only God can do, then your faith has to stretch toward Him.

When your need is attached to faith, it will move the Lord into action on your behalf. When you need a blessing, you will holler if you have to. She hollered at the Lord. Don't let go of the Lord, until you're lifted. Don't let go, until you're healed and restored. The woman hollered until the disciples, tried to shut her up. She hollered until hell started shaking. She hollered so much so, that her statement made the Lord holler. Jesus said, "O woman great is your faith, be it unto thee even as thou wilt."

As a result, her daughter was immediately healed. How bad do you want to be blessed? When you're too desperate to be denied, what you need God to do on your behalf will be done! Let your faith move God into action, to where He says, "O Woman, great is your faith!" Leave God no choice, but to bless you. He will break the rules, to work it out in your favor.

A WOMAN WITH AN ISSUE

Recorded in the Synoptic Gospels of Matthew, Mark, and Luke is the story of a woman with an issue of blood. It's interesting that her affliction was public, but her name was private. Imagine going through life, being known for what has been done to you and the negative experiences that you've had grapple through. Imagine being know as "The divorced woman" or "The woman with a dark past."

Would you want to be known as "The woman with the issue of abuse, neglect, or bad relationships?" Of course not! Your mess would override the essence, of the true message of your life. The stigma would affect your relationships. It would not make you feel good, about your life or yourself.

A particular passage in Matthew 9:20, 21 declares, "And, behold, a woman, which was diseased with an issue of blood twelve years, came behind Him (Jesus), and touched the hem of His garment. For she said within herself, If I may but touch His garment, I shall be whole."

The woman had an issue of blood, for 12 years. I believe if she was alive today, she would've had a starring role in the movie *12 Years a Slave*. For 12 years, she was a slave to her situation. You may not have the same particular issue that she had, but you might be grappling with a secret

issue. Oftentimes, we go through life broken, hurt, angry,

depressed, confused, and lacking love within ourselves.

I don't know what style of shoes she wore, but

imagine being in this woman's shoes. Under the law, she

was deemed to be unclean. She was not allowed to come in

contact with anybody or they would be classified, unclean

as well. Some people won't associate with you, because of

what someone said about you or how others view you.

Oftentimes, what we have experienced has made us

feel ashamed and unworthy. It causes our mindset and

self-esteem to be lowered. Yet in still, the woman pressed her

way through the crowd to Jesus. She wasn't even supposed to

be around all of those people, but she pressed her way

anyway. Can you press through the storm and the stress?

The Bible declares, "The woman said within herself."

What words are you saying to yourself? Are you saying that

you're a failure or a success? Are you thinking the worst or the best of yourself?

The woman didn't touch Jesus, but she touched something that was touching Him. She didn't touch Him, but she touched the hem of His garment. There was enough power in His garment, to transition her from sickness to healing. She had enough faith to push through her pain, to be free of the issue that kept her bound. What issue is affecting you? It doesn't matter how long, you've been carrying around your particular issue. If you bring it to God, He will handle it and empower you to live through it.

DADDY'S LITTLE GIRL

The journey of the woman with the issue of blood is situated, within the story of the daughter of Jairus (Matthew 9:18-24). His daughter has died, at twelve years of age. Imagine the grief felt, as daddy's little girl is no longer alive. Seemingly, she will never become the woman, that he envisioned her to be. I don't know how your relationship is with your father, but the bond between a daughter and her dad is uniquely significant. It affects a woman's relationships, particularly with men, for the rest of her life.

The woman with the issue of blood, had suffered for twelve years and we find Jairus' daughter dead at the age of twelve. How ironic. I would even suggest, that the woman with the issue of blood, was just as dead while being alive. To be existing and not living, is to be dead before dying.

WAKE UP

At age twelve, Jairus' daughter had lost her life. For the last twelve years, the woman with the issue of blood, was not able to live a normal life. Therefore, she was dead to herself and the people within her circle.

Jesus restored Jairus' daughter and the woman with the issue of blood, back to life. Before Jesus raised Jairus' daughter from the dead, he remarked "She is not dead, but is sleeping."

Only God can classify death, as an episode of sleep. I've got news for you, that your dream is not too dead for God to resurrect it. His hand of love is on your heart and He is awakening, the giant within you to rise and conquer. You've been sleeping too long, on your goals and dreams. God is resurrecting you to rise, walk in purpose, and destiny.

WOMAN OF WISDOM

When you're awakened, to the attributes and gifts that are within you, then you can walk as a woman of wisdom. Scripture declares in Proverbs 14:1, "Every wise woman buildeth her house: but the foolish plucketh it down with her hands." Being a woman of wisdom. is not conducive to age. It's a product of your stage of maturity. A wise woman builds her life, house, career, community, and her queendom.

A woman of wisdom, is resourceful. She can do more with less, because she's blessed. She builds and multiplies. Dr. Myles Munroe declared, "Whatever a woman receives she will multiply. Give her a word and she will give you a sentence. Give her a house and she will give you a beautiful home. Give her groceries and she will give you a delicious meal."

As a woman of wisdom, you were created to multiply because you are a resource who is resourceful. You have the right touch and whatever you put your hands to, will prosper. Nurture and multiply the gifts within you. Surround yourself with those who enhance, not diminish you. Yes, you're too wise to be a fool or surround yourself, with foolish people.

So many times, we blame "haters" for the situations we find ourselves in. When in fact, we created our own storms. If you create your own storm, then don't get mad when it rains. How can you point the blame at others, if you buried what you should have built? Use your hands to build your dream, rather than destroy it. Use your hands to build people's lives, instead of tear them down. Don't pluck, remove, or destroy your own blessings through negativity and self-destructive behaviors. God is increasing your level of wisdom, in order to make wise decisions. Don't get in the way, when God is trying to create a way for you.

THE POWER OF A PRAYING WOMAN

A pretty woman looks wonderful, but a praying woman is wonderful. She's a spiritual warrior! I know you're pretty and your bag is Gucci, but can you pray and seek the face of God earnestly? You can slay with the baddest of them, but can you pray somebody through bad times?

What would happen if you desired to slay spiritually, as much as you seek to do fashionably? In order to slay spiritually, you have to put on the whole armor of God.

Each day that you rise, there is a battle that you will face. Oftentimes, the battle is in your mind. You can't defeat the devil, unless you have the right weapons. Scripture declares, "For the weapons of our warfare are not carnal, but mighty through God to the pulling down of strong holds" (2 Corinthians 10:4). Only the weapon of God's Word, can give you the power to slay any attack of the enemy.

Dr. Martin Luther King, Jr. declared, "To be a Christian without prayer, is no more possible than to be alive without breathing." A prayer life, is essential to walk in the blessings of God for your life. You've had enough people, come into your life to prey on you. Begin to surround yourself, with those who will pray for you!

Your closet and wardrobe, should have more than a rack to hang clothes. It has to be a space, where you can reach God's throne. Your prayer closet, should create an atmosphere of praise and worship. Growing up in church, they would sing, "My mama prayed for me. She had me on her mind and took the time to pray for me. I'm so glad she prayed for me." Nothing is more powerful, than a woman's prayer. When women pray, they shake the very foundations of heaven. God honors your faith. He responds to your earnest cry and prayer concerning your son, daughter, finances, healing, career, relationships, and any issue that you face. When you remain prayed up, you clothe yourself with the whole armor of God, in order to slay the enemy and overcome adversity. Start preparing, for what you're praying to receive. Wake, pray, and slay each day.

Ephesians 6:14-17, reminds us about the spiritual war clothes needed to slay the enemy. You must have your loins, girt about with truth and put on the breastplate of righteousness. Your feet must be covered, with the preparation of the Gospel of peace. Take the shield of faith, the helmet of salvation, and the sword of the Spirit, which is

God's Word. You have all of this armor, but notice you don't have anything for your back. Simply because, God doesn't expect you to run from the enemy. He expects you, to put the devil on the run. You're armed and dangerous because "If you resist the devil, he will flee from you" (James 4:7). Your enemy is not your sister, it's the adversary who goes about as a "Roaring lion seeking whom he may devour" (I Peter 5:8). The devil desires, to devour your dreams and relationships. The enemy wants to steal, kill, and destroy your life. As a spiritual warrior, your faith will prevail beyond fear, because you possess the heart of a fighter.

PRAY AND SLAY

Just like the warrior, *Wonder Woman*, you've got power too. Warriors don't just get ready, they stay ready. How will you use the power within you? Will you use it for good or evil? Don't use your power to manipulate, hurt, and destroy lives. Stay prayed up, in these perilous times. The power of prayer is your weapon. Being to pray and slay sickness, sadness, cynicism, and sorrow. The enemy nor opposition stands a chance, when you're a praying woman whose armed and dangerous.

WOMB-MAN

As a woman, your womb is the place where life is generated and originated. God has partnered with you, to bring life into the world. God created heaven and earth, out of the dark womb of space. So too, has God given you a womb, that resembles the darkness of space, out of which everything is created and emanates. Your womb is God's workshop. Every leader, ruler, prophet, scientist, judge, and general came through the womb of a woman.

You are the centerpiece and star, of the spectacular phenomenon of created life. You are the median point, where humanity and divinity coalesce. Your womb is literally a gate. It is the portal from eternity into time. God used a woman, named Mary to bring Jesus into the world. Her womb carried the Savior, who brought the Word to the world.

Your womb is a beautiful birthing place, to manifest life. As long as the earth will stand, man will always be born of a woman. You are fearfully and wonderfully made. You were divinely designed, with a purpose in mind, to deliver your destiny. Whether you're plus size, midsize, or a small size, you must realize the riches that God has placed in you.

You were created to not only give life, but to nurture life. When little children fall and get hurt, they run past everybody to get to mama because she's a nurturer. It's fine to nurture as a parent, but it's a terrible thing to nurture pain. If you don't deal with and heal from the pain, it will take root deep down inside of you. As a result, you will keep alive what should have died and hold on to, what you should have let go.

Know that between the promise and the product, is a

process. Right between the revelation and manifestation, is your situation. God wants to birth something new even now. Stop birthing things, that God doesn't want you to produce. Stop birthing dead relationships and then trying to resuscitate them. You will only birth out of you, that which is within you.

You had a child and your womb is empty of life, but now filled with pain. What is in your womb, that's wounding you? Don't allow negativity to occupy the space, where only positivity should flow from. You can't continue holding on to guilt and nursing grief. The jewel can't be birthed, if your womb is filled with junk. Don't fill your womb with worry. Fill it with worship. Scripture declares, "Out of your belly shall flow rivers of living water" (John 7:38). Not just streams and lakes, but rivers of riches and righteousness.

Let God place in you, what He wants to birth through you. Make room for your womb, to bloom and birth the business. Make room for your womb, to birth fruitful relationships, transform contacts into contracts, and ideas into income. Your womb is not a tomb for death, disease, destruction, despair, and discombobulated thoughts to reside. Your womb is a place for life, legacy, and leadership to flow through you. The womb that was abused, God will use to birth healing. Your womb may harbor pain, the loss of a child, incest, fornication, or an illicit affair. Still, God can heal it, so you can push out your purpose and reveal it.

Stop crying over the man who left and get excited about the one, who is coming. Don't lose your mind over your past, because you're going to need your mind to walk into your future. Stop crying over the house you lost. Start rejoicing, over the bigger one that's coming. Stop crying, complaining, and grieving. Begin praising God through it.

The worst is over! The bad season of your life has officially ended. The grief, hardship, sadness, sorrow, depression, and thoughts of suicide are over. God is doing a new thing in your life. For "Old things are passed away, behold all things are become new" (II Corinthians 5:7). The word "behold" means to look. Open your eyes of faith and look at your joy. Look at your strength. Look at your resilience and see your beauty within. The best and blessed is yet to come.

This is your season to deliver the promise, that God has placed in you. God is making room in your womb, for what He designed you to deliver. It's time to push out, your dream and vision. Push through everything, that pushed you down and hindered you. Birth a beautiful breakthrough from brokenness. Your womb will birth wisdom, from your wounds. As a *Wonder Woman*, expect God to birth something wonderful in your life!

CHAPTER 12

Woman Thou Art Loosed

*When you're loosed, what bound and broke you,
now becomes your breakthrough to be blessed.*

I was recently honored, to be an empowerment speaker

at Bishop T.D. Jakes' *MegaFest*. More than 50,000 men and

women descended upon Dallas, Texas to be empowered and

inspired spiritually, relationally, and economically. It was

mega! So many people were mega blessed at *MegaFest*.

WOMAN TO WOMAN

Yes, I was humbled to be included and invited, but even

more so enamored, by the camaraderie that commenced

from woman to woman. Uniqueness was displayed in a mega

way, via shapes, sizes, nationalities, and personalities. One could see that differences, don't equate to deficiencies. Diversity is not adversity, but strength when actualized. In the midst of diversity, there was a common language expressed that every woman could convey to the other. Seemingly, they didn't have to know each other, to know each other. From woman to woman, there was an enriching sisterhood that was communicated and conveyed.

I'M EVERY WOMAN

The subtle gesture expressed was a smile, compliment, or comment such as "Girl, I like those shoes. Your hair looks good or this is amazing." In one place there was every kind of woman, who came with expectation to receive a mega blessing. Not just for herself, but for family, friends, and sisters who were joined together.

Chaka Khan and Whitney Houston beautifully sang the words, "I'm every woman. It's all in me. Anything you want done, baby I'll do it naturally." Your beauty, femininity, and identity is designed so uniquely. Even in your distinct differences, your uniqueness makes you every *WOMAN* because you **W**onderfully **O**rchestrate **M**agnanimous **A**chievements **N**aturally!

Even in my admiration of you, I admonish you to surround yourself with sisters who support you. A real sister, is her sister's keeper. She won't hate on you. She will celebrate, elevate, and empower you. She doesn't desire to compete, she intends to collaborate. Real sisters see the best in you and want the best for you. Real sisters, queens, and women are every woman, just like you.

YOU GO GIRL!

The phrase "You go girl" was popularized on the hit comedy show *Martin*, starring Martin Lawrence and Tisha Campbell. When Martin gave his girlfriend Gina, a compliment or motivation, he would say, "You go girl" with enthusiasm!

God is aligning you with people, who are for you. People who are pro your vision, will empower you to receive provision. You don't need pseudo, so-called sisters in your circle who bring drama, jealousy, and strife. You will find yourself singing like Bell Biv DeVoe, "That girl is poison!" Remove the poisonous people out of your life, that limit your next level. Some people don't want you to grow, if they aren't growing themselves. Surround yourself with people who enhance your growth, not the ones who stunt it.

If you don't have people in your life who affirm you, look in the mirror and affirm yourself. Learn how to encourage yourself. Give yourself a pat on the back. Tell yourself how beautiful you are. Tell yourself how amazing your life will become.

Everything you've been through, was preparation for where God is taking you. He wants you to grow and go to the next level. Surround yourself with people who aren't intimidated and celebrate your success, when you go to the next level. People who are intimidated, will eventually be eliminated from your space.

A man who is not intimidated by you, wants to see you shine and will bring out the best in you. He will holler like Martin and say, "You go girl!" Go and get your degree. Go and open the business. Go and write the book. Go and start the non-profit organization. Go and step into ministry. Go and be the best, that you can be. On your mark, get set, go!

WOMEN ARE FROM VENUS

You have heard countless times, "Men are from Mars and women are from Venus." The statement highlights that men and women, don't always understand each other, as they are seemingly from two different planets. It's not so much about deficiencies, as it is differences. The splendiferous and appealing pulchritude of a woman, can enrapture and permeate any man's mind. However, I don't think you could write enough books or do enough research, to explain and figure out the psyche of a woman. I'm sure you feel the same way about men.

Indeed, there is nothing more splendid than to see the glow in a woman's eyes being surprised, when you give her roses or a gift. On the contrary, nothing is more scathing than to see the fiery eyes of a woman scorned.

WAFFLES AND SPAGHETTI

Someone expressed, that men are like waffles and women are like spaghetti. Besides being hungry now, the real hunger pangs, derive emotionally due to a lack of continuity.

The small walled boxes on the edges of waffles, symbolize a man's mental compartmentalization. On the other hand, the overlapping nature of spaghetti, symbolizes a woman's psychological interconnection. A man tends to block things out and bring things in his life, by focusing on facts and not emotions. Women are generally feeling oriented and express their emotions more readily than men. You are stronger communicators and maybe you're thinking, you're smarter than us too.

Since men have been socialized to be super strong, oftentimes vulnerability and masculinity, cannot coexist in the same space. Simply because in society, vulnerability is viewed as femininity, rather than true masculinity.

Oftentimes as men, we don't verbalize rather we internalize our emotions. We suppress, what you express. As men, we have been socialized to push through pain. No pain, no gain. We are conditioned, to show no form of weakness. We release it, dismiss it, disconnect, and disassociate from who or what caused it.

On the contrary, women are like spaghetti. If you notice, every noddle in the bowl overlaps. Some women overlap, mix, and intertwine their life experiences, both good and bad. The experiences in the past, are presently affecting you now. Some women will talk about the hurt, from a relationship that happened five years ago, as if it just happened five minutes ago. The experiences overlap one another. If you continue to harbor hurt, it will continue to hold on to you.

As a man, we have a tendency of letting things go arguably easier than you. If we cry, it's not for long. Yes, men do cry in the dark, but where do we go to shed light on our issues if all we're taught to be is hypermasculine? How do you open up, if you're only socialized to keep the emotional door closed?

So we dry our eyes, hide the pain, keep working, hang out with the fellas for a minute, and press toward the prize. However, many men don't heal, because they choose to ignore the real hurt and pain on the inside.

A FEW GOOD MEN

The movie, *A Few Good Men* is more than a drama film. In many cases, it evokes life's drama script that plays out. The widening ratio of women to men, is quite visible in many places around the world. However, more than just getting a man, you naturally want companionship and compatibility with an eligible suitor. Beyond quantity, you desire quality.

Most women will affirm, when they were girls they got better grades than the boys in their classes. I'm sure your paper was the cheat sheet. We may have bigger biceps, but it's argued that you have the brighter brain. Since the late 1970s, women outnumber men on college campuses and steadily graduate at a greater rate than men do. Female graduates account, for roughly 60% of U.S. bachelor's degree holders. Girls mature three years quicker than boys and even when we reach adulthood, many women will say that we still haven't caught up. On average, you live longer.

According to *The New England Centenary*, of all the people in the world who are older than 100, 85% of them are women. A study by McGill University, indicated that a woman's immune system is stronger than a man's. Estrogen gives women an edge, when it comes to fighting off infections. You're charitable as a caregiver, 36% of women take care of their elderly parents. Only 16% of men do that. The average woman reads nine books a year, compared to only five for men. Glad to know mine is one of them.

Research indicates, that women are better at multitasking as opposed to men. Only you can make macaroni and cheese, apply makeup, and map out your schedule, all at the same time. Many religious services are comprised of more women than men, being 61% female and 39% male. In a seminar I jokingly said, "I think men are the rough draft and women are the finally copy." However, what's not a joke, is where do you find "a few good men" if you're always outnumbering them?

Isaiah 4:1 declares, "In that day so few men will be left that seven women will fight for each man, saying, Let us all marry you! We will provide our own food and clothing. Only let us take your name so we won't be mocked as old maids." Scripture highlights the wide ratio of women to men. We see it in communities and on TV shows, where multiple women fight for a man, who won't fight for them. As a result, the women who want the man, won't even require him to support them. They simply want a man for optics, protection, companionship, and validation. The desire and need for it, causes many to lower their standards to receive it.

GROWN BOY

Today we see many women, providing for a grown boy without a job, who should provide for you and himself. If he can't provide for himself, what makes you think he will provide for you? It's one thing to support a man when he's struggling, but it's another thing to support someone who only wants to leech off you. Something is wrong if he's living in your house and eating your food, but won't put you in a house or provide you with the basic necessities. So, he's driving your car, to pick you up from work? You were not created to provide for a man. He was created to provide for you. God didn't even create a woman and place her on this planet, until everything was provided.

A grown woman will always be frustrated, dealing with a grown boy who won't man up. No wonder you're frustrated and tired. You're supposed to be with a man, who has a vision. He's supposed to pray for you, provide, and protect you. However, the roles are now reversed. It used to be hardworking men and pretty women. Now men want to look pretty, while women work hard. We see women going in search of husbands, rather than men searching for wives. All to remove the supposed shame or stigma, of being

WOMAN - Dr. Eddie Connor

unmarried. It's not worth it to settle. Married doesn't always mean you're happy and single doesn't mean you're miserable. You can still live a blessed life, until your time comes to be a wife. Don't live your life to get another man's name, especially if he doesn't know who he is as a man. If you don't know the essence of your name and nature as a woman, taking his name won't make a difference.

CONDITIONED FOR COMPANIONSHIP

I find it interesting, that a woman can be married in her mind or in "the spirit." I've heard some women say, "He's my husband, but he just don't know it yet." So he's not yours, but "he's yours?"

Some women will take it further and say, "God told me to tell you, that you're my husband." Well, the problem is that God didn't tell me, what you're saying He told you. So, tell Him to tell me and then I'll know what He told you!

Men don't operate like that. First and foremost we're visual. Beyond spiritual, what's not physical or tangible won't be marital! As men, our structure and concepts of relationships are far different than yours. Since you were a little girl, you have been conditioned for companionship all of your life.

You danced with dolls, playing with Barbie and Ken. As a child, you dressed each of them for the wedding and sang, "Here comes the bride." You even performed the wedding yourself. Your play partners, were dolls in full-length wedding dresses at the age of four. You knew what dress you wanted to wear, at your wedding when you were fifteen. Your prom dress was the prelude, to the wedding dress that you envisioned yourself wearing. Ever since you were a child, you were conditioned for companionship.

Most men were not raised and socialized as you are. We grew up playing sports outside and video games inside. We collected rocks, comic books, baseball, and basketball cards. We played and fought with action figures, while you danced with dolls. Are dolls and games, a foreshadow of what's to come? In many cases, she goes through life manipulating mates like dolls. He continues to play games and his heart is as hard, as the rocks he collected.

BARBIE AND KEN

Could it be that you're going through life, looking for a Ken but you still keep meeting the wrong kind? Some women treat a man like a Ken doll, by trying to manipulate and control him. You can move his head, hands, and feet by the sway of your hips. You know how to woo him and get him to do, what you want him to do. Whatever you have to manipulate to get, you will have to manipulate to keep. Ultimately, you will lose it and yourself in the process. The greatest tool you have is not between your legs, it's between your ears. A real man wants to know what's in your mind, not just see your behind. If he's not worthy of having you, then he's not worth having you.

Just like a Ken doll, he has a car, house, and career. However, he has no mind to think and no heart to love. A Ken doll has everything externally, but it lacks the main resources internally. It lacks a mind to rationalize and a heart to love. Turning his head means nothing, if he doesn't have a heart.

Too often the subtle appeal, is to make women aspire to be like Barbie who isn't real. You focus on your body, but not your mentality. Struggling with issues of image and self-identity. You change your hair color, but still feel the same. You focus on what's external, but not internal. As a result, you look beautiful on the outside but lack love for yourself on the inside. Don't allow society to deceive you, with a pseudo portrayal of how to perceive yourself. Never let stereotypical images alter the way you receive, the essence of who you are as a woman. Appreciate, love yourself, and celebrate who you are, so a generation of young girls can embrace womanhood naturally.

Barbie and Ken dolls are fake and phony. You don't need a mannequin, you need a man again. A real man can think for himself. He will lead, lift, and love you, without being controlled or manipulated by you.

The significance of your success, is not in having somebody. Don't put your power in the hands of people. Don't listen to people who rush you and tell you, "Hurry up and get married." If you're not careful, you will settle for anybody to satisfy those saying you don't have somebody.

HEAD, HEART, HANDS

Oftentimes, there is a dichotomy between your head and your

heart. They are on two different paths and rarely converge. Your head says, "I don't need him." However, your heart is saying, "I want him." It's a constant battle. If the Lord doesn't put His hands on your head and heart, then you will drive yourself crazy. Begin to pray, for the Lord to renew your spirit and mind. Your spirit has to be in control of your mind, in order to control the emotions of your heart. If not, you will desire who you shouldn't be with and extend your hands to the wrong person. A renewed mind, will bring about a renewed focus.

If your mind is conformed and not transformed, you will have last year's experience this time next year. The hardest thing to do, is to have God pull you out of what your flesh likes. Sometimes you're so comfortable dealing with drama, that you don't even realize it's slowly killing you.

Has God ever pulled you out of a situation, that you like? It was no good for you and you knew it. God told you.

Your mama told you, your sister told you, your brother told you, friends told you, and the pastor told you. Even the one you were with told you, but you wouldn't listen. All of that advice and you refused to listen, because you had to have what you wanted. You thought you could change the person. It's easy to get over what you don't want, but it's hard to get over what you do want. Even when it's not good for you.

It's just like fried chicken, chips, candy, burgers, pizza, soda, and fries. The food tastes good, but it clogs your arteries. It leads to increased weight gain, raises your blood pressure, lowers energy, and leads to high cholesterol. It tastes good to you, but in the long run it's not good for you. The food that tastes the best, often has the worst effects on your body.

Much like the relationship, they looked good to you but weren't any good for you. The more you got involved the more headaches and heartache you had, because drama was the side effect. Junk food and junk relationships, are bad for your health and well-being. Change your habits and get them out of your diet. This time if you let God choose, then you will never lose.

SINGLE, SAVED, SANCTIFIED, SATISFIED

Single means to be whole, not broken, or separated. Learn how to be whole, before you get married and not just because you are married. If you're incomplete before them, you will be depleted after them. A man loving you doesn't matter, if you don't love yourself.

Take the time to genuinely love yourself. Cook for yourself. Exponentially increase your self-respect and self-esteem. Pamper yourself as a whole woman and you will attract a whole man. One whole woman, will attract one whole man and create one whole marriage. A half woman can't love a whole man. Your brokenness will only attract broken people, who fully mistreat you and half love you.

A half person will only attract a half person, never being whole and complete. Some people don't want love, they want help. They have a hand out to take, but nothing to give. They live a half-hearted lifestyle, only giving half effort. You're only going to get a half marriage, from a half person. Walk in the wholeness that God has for you, so He can give you, who He has for you.

When you're thirsty for the wrong thing, you will end up accepting and settling for anything. When you're dissatisfied you surround yourself with different bodies, to make you feel like somebody. You really need love, but you'll settle for sex, in hopes that your thirst can be quenched.

A need that's left unaddressed, is a dangerous thing. A need will make you operate out of desperation. When they say, "Desperate times call for desperate measures" they didn't lie. People who are needy, will go to desperate measures and great lengths, because of the magnitude of their thirst. When you're needy and thirsty, you will settle to be someone's "wife" for the weekend. When you're needy and thirsty, you will settle for being a side chick. As a result, never finding the love you're void of to quench it.

You can live a victorious life and be a virtuous wife. You don't have to lower your standards, for the sake of having somebody. A person cannot fill the void in your life or make you happy, if you're not happy with yourself. When you're not happy, you can't make anybody else happy. You can't give anybody anything, that you don't have. If you didn't get any love or affirmation, you can't give it. In most cases, you will refuse to receive it.

Have you ever tried to keep somebody in a state of happiness, who wasn't happy with themselves? Yes, I know it's frustrating. They will put you through changes, have you jumping through hoops, and now your hair is turning gray.

Sadly, some people are only happy, when you're hurting. If helping you is hurting me, then you're not the right one for me. The worst thing is to be crying, while someone is rejoicing about your pain. The tables will turn in your favor. While you're crying, God is wiping your tears and healing you from within.

If you're not qualified to be by yourself, then you're not qualified to be with me. You can't expect anybody to make you happy, if you can't make yourself happy. Stop running from person to person, to find satisfaction. Your spiritual satisfaction is more important, than a physical interaction. I know you're waiting to exhale, but the wrong one will make you suffocate and bring you hell.

Have you ever considered, that God can satisfy you? Deep within, do you really believe that He can? God can take the messy, broken, and wounded issues in your life, by blessing, touching, and healing you from every infirmity.

Whether you're alone or in a one bed room apartment, He can satisfy you. For all the people who disappointed you, God is getting ready to surprise and satisfy you. He will empower you, so that the joy of the Lord is your strength.

ALL IS WELL

A man, money, cars, clothes, career, and possessions will pacify you, but it won't satisfy you. Just like the woman at the well, only God can quench your thirsty soul. The spiritual satisfaction that God places in your soul, will make you look at your situation and declare all is well. When you feel depressed, desperate or in a drought, the well of God's living water will spring up within you. The living water of the Lord, will be a well that springs up in your soul. For out of your belly, shall flow rivers of living water (John 7:38). Despite the heartache and hell, you will say, "All is well!"

FINISH THE PUZZLE

People are always inquisitive, about my writing process. It's my eighth book, so I'm not new to this. I'm true to this. Some suggest how in the world, do I have time and how do I make time to write a book? Well, you always make time for what you want. Especially, when it's your gift and passion. To me, writing a book is like a puzzle. Generally, my mind is moving faster than my fingers can type and ideas are coming from all directions, at lightning speed. The words are the puzzle pieces and the finished book becomes the frame.

Sometimes life becomes like a puzzle, as we try to find the missing pieces to make our lives whole. Your faith may be fragmented. Even your next move may seem puzzling, as the enemy seeks to muzzle your praise. Be encouraged through it all, because God will guide you through the process.

On the flip side, you may have all of the pieces except

that last one. You have the car, the credit score, the house, and career, but you're missing that lasting relationship. Stop looking for the last piece and let God reveal it. Don't force puzzle pieces together, that weren't meant to fit in your life. The right fit, is not a counterfeit. Let God finish the puzzle of your life, so he can fit together what is meant for you. Hand him the pieces of your life and He will make all things new.

WASHED WOMAN

It's interesting, how I arrived at the title of this book. I never rush my writing, for the sake of writing something. If it's not authentic, I don't want to be in it.

One day, I was routinely touching up my beard in the bathroom and began to wash my hands in the sink. All of a sudden, the title *Woman* dropped in my mind and I couldn't shake it. Wherever I went, I kept thinking about the title of the book. I pondered about the kind of woman, this book is uniquely designed to empower.

Symbolically as I washed my hands, I believe it's a reminder that God has washed your sins away. He's washing away the hurt, pain, blemishes, bitterness, and brokenness in your life. The dirt, discombobulation, and frustration is all being washed and wiped away. You're a woman, whose been washed in the blood of the lamb. As God is cleaning you up, He's also picking you up and elevating you. God is lifting you, to a place that's greater than your past. He is elevating you above haters and traitors. God is strengthening you, to transform weakness into greatness.

THIS MEANS WAR

When the enemy is after your children, your marriage, your ministry, your home, your finances, your family, and your life, then this means war! Get up and fight. Take back your life in Jesus' name! You can't help where you've been, but you can help where you're going. You may have been knocked down, but don't stay down. Get up! Get back in the fight and overcome every enemy of adversity. God will release His favor to win and give you strength to fight. Whatever you're going through, remember the fight is fixed. The battle belongs to the Lord and in the end, you win!

THE WAILING WOMAN

The devil is afraid and hates for women, to come together and collaborate with each other. Something powerful happens when women work together, pray together, believe together, and build together. The enemy despises it and wants you to fall out, about silly disputes over shoes, hats, whose dating who, whose married, who thinks they're cute, or who you think is after your husband. You being pretty doesn't scare the enemy. The devil wants you to be petty.

The enemy doesn't want you to touch and agree. For one can chase a thousand, but two can chase ten thousand

(Deuteronomy 32:30). Too many people have touched you to disagree, but God is sending the right sisters to touch and agree with you for breakthrough. Imagine what would happen if you connected with your sisters, instead of conspiring against them? Now that's real girl power! Imagine the great wonders that would take place, when women work and worship together!

Jeremiah 9:17 declares, "Consider and call for the mourning women, that they may come; And send for the wailing women, that they may come." The word "wailing" means to feel deep sorrow. It means to cry, groan, and lament. When the Lord begins to call for women, it's because emergency intervention is needed. The situation has become so dire, that only the prayers of a woman can bring deliverance. Look at our world and the perilous times, that we live in. The hearts of people have grown cold. The world lacks love as violence, turmoil, and wickedness increases.

A man's strength can't always do, what a woman's subtle sensitivity can speak to. In your sensitivity is strength. God hears the pain in a woman's cry. The earnest cry within your soul, has a higher pitch and depth that moves God expediently on your behalf. The climate of the world we live in, needs daughters of destiny to come together and pray in desperate times. Psalm 126:5 declares, "They that sow in tears shall reap in joy." Your tears are watering the seeds for your harvest. How many tears have you shed over loved ones, the hurt you experienced, and the trials you faced? Even when you don't have the words to express, God can understand the inarticulate tears that fall from your eyes.

THANK YOU CARD

Don't sulk another minute, over a marred marriage that didn't work. Don't get depressed over a ragged relationship, that was ruined. Don't be bitter and upset at your ex, because it's positioning you for what's next. The next book, the next career, the next relationship, and the next journey. The ex was an example, of how to find opportunity from adversity. Don't be bitter, get better. The sadness isn't a setback, it's a setup for gladness. Shake off the negative thoughts and crippling ideas in your mind. Stop remaining under, what you have the power to get over. Put on your best dress, makeup, and earrings. On your journey, hop in the passengers seat. This time let Jesus take the wheel, to drive you into destiny.

In everything give thanks. Send the person in your mind, a thank you card. Tell them, "Thank you for hurting me, because it made me stronger to walk in healing. Thank you for cursing me out, because now I know what encouraging words sound like. Thank you for deceiving me, because I learned how to trust in God. Thank you for wounding me, because wisdom now flows through me. You abused me, but now God is using me." This is your hallmark moment. Make an indelible mark that can't be erased.

God brought you through, because He has something greater for you. He has something BIG, in store for you. It's greater than where you've been. It's greater than what you've seen and achieved. It's higher than where you've reached. It's above, what you've ever thought of and conceptualized. Reach for it! Why do you think you're still alive? Why do you think, you've kept your mind? Other women have gone through, what you've been through and didn't survive. You're still here! You're still alive! Now it's time to thrive. Don't you dare give up! God is about to elevate you to a divine dimension.

TOO LOOSED, TO BE BOUND

Jesus told the crippled woman in Luke 13:12, "Woman thou art loosed." Confess over your life, that you're loosed from abuse, loosed from your past, loosed from the pain of brokenness, loosed from low self-esteem, loosed from depression, bitterness, and anger. You are loosed to walk in liberty and love!

THE CRIPPLED WOMAN

In Luke chapter 13, the woman in the story could not straighten her body, look upward, or forward. Her body, was bent toward the ground for 18 years. Imagine having to walk bent over, for 18 years, much less 18 minutes. It's painful.

Now, I've had back pains on a number of occasions and if your body is bent over, then you know it feels horrendous. However, it's another thing to deal with an infirmity for 18 years.

As it was, she could only see the dirt at her feet. She could only look downward and see the bad side of things. She could not look up and see the possibilities before her. She could not see the smiles on people's faces. She could not see the beautiful light, that permeates from the clouds. She could only look down to the ground.

Sometimes life brings you so low, that all you trust is the dust. Life can deal you a bad hand, to where you become pessimistic instead of optimistic. Despite what you have experienced, shake it off. Just because it's been that way, doesn't mean it will stay that way. You can change your circumstance, by thinking positive in a negative situation.

HEAVY HEART, HEAVY ISSUES

Can you imagine this woman? She could only look down, because she was bent over. Sometimes issues weigh us down so heavily, that our physical body is impacted. How we feel on the inside, will impact our body and expression on the outside.

Whatever is going on in your mind, will manifest throughout your body. You can only smile through pain, for so long before you breakdown. They say, "Fake it, until you make it." However, you truly won't make it, if you have to fake it. Rather, "Faith it, until you make it." Believe and walk by faith. When you become real with your issues, you will seek relief. It takes getting tired, of being sick and tired, to find healing.

ANSWER THE CALL

When Jesus saw her condition, the Bible said, "He called her to Him." Even in the midst of your chaos, Jesus is calling you closer to Him. Don't let worry, put a wedge between you and God. You moved closer to people and they left you in a worse condition, than before you met them. They crippled you, but God will restore you. Focus and move closer to Him, not them. God wants to speak to you. So get close to Him, so you can hear from Him. Will you answer His call?

FROM SICKNESS TO WHOLENESS

The woman was crippled but Jesus declared, "Woman, thou art loosed from thine infirmity." He told her that she was free. She was free from the infirmity, that twisted her body into a deformed shape. The woman immediately straightened her body and was made whole. Just like Jesus straightened up the woman, He is also straightening up your life. He is healing you, so that you can lift up your head with confidence. He is loosing you, so that you can live a life of abundance. He is strengthening your mind, body, and spirit, so that you can walk in your purpose and share your testimony.

Jesus didn't tell the woman, that she was about to be loosed. She was already free, when He spoke healing. As you're reading, God is loosing you from every infirmity. Walk like it, talk like it, act like it, and live like it. The situation that crippled you last time, can't hold you this time.

You're not going to lose your mind. God will loose your mind for the next level! Jesus didn't focus on the woman's sickness, He highlighted her wholeness. God wants you to be whole. He doesn't want your faith fragmented and your mind discombobulated. He wants you to be made whole and loosed to live an abundant life.

LET HIM USE YOU

When "abuse" is transformed, it becomes "use." If anybody is going to use you, let it be God. If you let God loose you, He can use you. Let Him use you, to tell your testimony and uplift somebody. You may have had an abortion, but God didn't abort your purpose. He didn't throw you away, because of the trials you went through. You may have been abused, but God can still use you.

There is no hurt, that God can't heal. There is no pain, that He can't feel. Yes, you may have been raped, but you can still reap a blessing. Your weeping is releasing a blessing.

268

The breaking point, will become your breakthrough. There is healing, despite the pain you're experiencing.

The molestation that you experienced, was designed to rob you of your self-esteem. The situation is being used, for greater preparation to perfect greatness in you. God is going to restore what someone stole. Don't give up. Don't die in it, but live through dying places. A great testimony is coming out of it. God will heal and fill the void through it.

You know what it's like, to come home full after a great meal, but still feel empty. You roll over in the middle of the night, desiring to be held, but only sadness has you in its grip. Your innocence was violated. As a result, you don't trust men. Now, it keeps you bitter, sad, angry, hostile, negative, promiscuous, and cold as the winter. The devil knows, if you are whole, you will be dangerous and walk in your destiny. Be encouraged! What was designed to break you down, God will turn it around and use it to break you through.

He has not forgotten you. God isn't looking for a woman, that's got it all together. All of your flaws and imperfections are perfect enough. God doesn't call qualified people. He qualifies the people He calls. God doesn't take an opinion poll from people, to see if He will bless you or not. God will veto any vote against you. Rather, He uses who He chooses and your strength, is made perfect in weakness. Be loosed from what's holding you bound. No more bondage, it's time for you to breakthrough.

You've been through too much, to stay where you are now. You're stronger than you think. You're wiser than you realize. When God is on your side, you can't be denied. Woman thou art loosed! Come out of your cave, come out of your abuse. Come out of sorrow, sadness, sickness, and thoughts of suicide!

READY OR NOT, HERE I COME

When I was a kid, we would play "Hide-and-seek." The last

thing I would say after counting was, "Ready or not, here I come." Tell every enemy and situation, those same words. Step out with your talent. Come forth with your gifts. The world is waiting, for you to come out of hiding. The anointing that God gave you, bring it out. Shine and share it. God has opened the door and it's your time to come out!

Never hide, what God put His glow inside. Come out with new vision. Come out with greater joy. Come out with a fresh anointing. Give every hater, a front row seat to your success. Don't let people decide, how your life should work. Stop riding in the back seat of your life. Let God take the wheel, so you don't crash into your past.

LOOSED TO LIVE

You're on the hit list of hell, because the devil is afraid of what you will do to lift God's kingdom. The enemy knows that if you ever get on your feet and recognize your royalty, then you will walk in your destiny.

Ever since you were a child, the devil tried to destroy you and initiate generational curses on your life. The enemy wanted your home life, your family, and your background to be in complete chaos. The enemy wanted your life, to be in such disarray that you would lack affection, self-esteem, nurturing, security, healthy relationships, or the stability to become what God created you to be. The devil is a liar!

To have made it through, what you've been through is nothing short of a miracle. God has greater in store for you! You're still here and in your right mind, because God has a purpose in mind for your life. You're coming out, because you're loosed to live! Even as you're reading, God is healing you from every infirmity, insecurity, and skewed identity.

When God shows you what He wants you to be, it's generally who you aren't already. Even now, what God is showing you, is an example of what He's already placed in you. God is peeling away the layers of pain, mistakes, abuse, resentment, anger, shame, struggle, tests, trials, insecurity, and negative thoughts.

When you get loosed, everything around you will be loosed. You're loosed to love. You're loosed to live. You're loosed to give. You're loosed from negative thinking. You're loosed from the noose of abuse. You're loosed from mistreatment. You're loosed from low self-esteem. You're loosed from debt, doubt, and a defeated lifestyle. Woman thou art loosed in Jesus' name! I loose your house. I loose your spouse. I loose your marriage. I loose you. I loose you to be a woman of love, truth, and strength.

LOOSED AND BLESSED

God is not through with you. He has loosed you, for a greater purpose. When you're loosed, what bound and broke you, now becomes your breakthrough to be blessed. You're loosed from confusion. Loosed from fear. Loosed from every scar and struggle. You're loosed to walk in healing. You're loosed to love. You're loosed to live. You're loosed to forgive. You're loosed to have life more abundantly. If you have to cry, crawl, and drag yourself out of the mess, come out by any means necessary. You may have went in limping, but come out leaping and rejoicing. It's your time to be loosed.

As a result of being loosed, now you're blessed! *Woman*, thou art blessed and highly favored. You're loosed and blessed, to be a CEO. You're loosed and blessed, to bring unity to your community. You're loosed and blessed, to be whole in your singleness. You're loosed and blessed, to be a wife and mother. You're loosed and blessed, to be a spouse who brings love in the house. You're loosed, to lose a bad attitude. You're loosed, to shake off abuse. You're loosed and blessed, to find beauty in brokenness. You're loosed and blessed, to transform every wound into wisdom.

O *Woman*, great is your faith! Hold fast to your blessing and God's Word of healing. His Word will deliver you. His Word speaks to your innermost needs, your fears, and tears. God even speaks to your gender, in a tender way.

Open your spiritual ears. Listen closely and intently. His Word speaks life and liberty, to your secret thoughts and self-esteem. God is breaking the chains of your past and removing limitations, from your future. *Woman* there is nothing that has happened to you, that God can't see you through. There is no hurt, that God can't handle and heal. He will wipe away your tears. He will exchange it for courage, to face your fears.

God has loosed you from darkness, to walk in His marvelous light. Stand up straight. Look to the hills from where your help comes, because the Lord is lifting you. His elevation, is lifting you above your situation. You're now free, to walk in the light of liberty. Break free, from the prison of your past and march into the freedom of your future. Move from your history, into your destiny. Build a legacy, as you walk in victory. Stretch your faith and focus. Spread your wings and soar like an eagle, to elevate to the next level because *WOMAN* thou art loosed!

You go girl! You're focused and *FINE*: *Feminine Intelligent, Nurturing,* and *Empowered*. It's your time shine! It's your season to recover and discover wisdom from your wounds. Shake yourself. Follow God's pace and run your race. You are His leading lady. You are a divine daughter of destiny. You're a queen of quality. Love yourself.

Walk in your value, virtue, and royalty. Let your strength show and let your beauty glow. Birth your greatness. Wear your crown! Continue to *Wonderfully Orchestrate Magnanimous Achievements Naturally*. Celebrate and embrace your beauty, femininity, royalty, destiny, and personal identity, as an extraordinary *WOMAN!*

IT'S IN YOUR HANDS

I can't end this book without a story. It details a young girl, who desired to outwit an old woman. You know, most young people think they know everything and older people don't think they can learn anything new. However, as comedian Kevin Hart would say, "You're gonna learn today."

One day, a young girl dashed across the street to capture a small and fragile bird. After picking up the bird, she placed it behind her back. She decided in her young mind, that she would confound an old woman's wisdom with a simple question. So, the girl walked with the bird behind her back, toward the old woman and said, "Ma'am, is the bird that I'm holding behind my back, dead or alive?" The young girl already made up in her mind, that if the old woman replied, "It's dead" she would release it, so it can fly away. However, if the old woman said, "It's alive" she would crush the bird and kill it.

So, the old woman begins to ponder the question, "Is the bird dead or alive?" As the old woman thinks to herself, she presses her glasses against her face, brushes her hair from her eyes, and props her fragile frame up on her walking cane. The old woman clears her throat, looks at the young girl, and says, "My dear, the answer is in your hands."

As you're reading, begin realizing that the power of forgiveness, is in your hands. The power of love, is in your hands. The answer to clean up your community and bring unity, is in your hands. The answer to silence the violence, is in your hands. The business plan, is in your hands. Your creativity, ingenuity, integrity, dream, vision, and destiny is in YOUR hands. What will you do with it? Will you kill it, release it, or build a bright future with it?

The other day, I was looking for my glasses and they were on my face. I was moving so fast, that I was looking for my phone and it was on my ear. I was looking for my watch and it was on my wrist. Oftentimes, we go through life looking for what we already have in us and on us. Stop looking around you, for what you already have within you. Stop looking for love on the outside, when love begins on the inside. Open your eyes and see your wealth within.

So many people, are in a hurry going nowhere. Stop moving so fast. Slow down. Assess, invest, and take the time to do some personal inventory within yourself. As you look within, you will see that everything you've been looking for, was always looking back at you. You are the leader, that you were looking for all along. Too often we look, for what we already have. We ask God to give us, what we already possess. Stir your gifts and galvanize your greatness. Realize who you are and recognize what is in your hands.

PERSONAL INVENTORY

In order to recognize what you have, you must take the time to assess and invest in yourself. If not you, then who else will? Take the time to be introspective about your spirit, health, well-being, mentality, and relationships.

1. What are three principles conveyed in this book, that you can apply as a blueprint, to build your life?

a.

b.

c.

2. Beyond your makeup, nails, heels, the clothes you wear, style of your hair, and what you own...what are some qualities that make you a quintessential *Woman*?

3. How will you transform the 10% struggle of your life, into total strength?

4. What will you do daily, to ensure your spiritual growth?

5. Your peace of mind is pertinent, to your fulfillment and happiness in life. What will you do, to ensure your mental health daily? (Example: meditating, reading, etc.)

6. Your health is your wealth. Exercise and nutrition are essential building blocks, to longevity of life. How will you improve your fitness and healthy food intake? Describe your plan and write your goals below:

7. What is the ultimate vision for your life? What are you doing now, to maximize your potential and bring your vision to fruition?

8. Greatness begins by serving others. As you're leading, who are you helping and serving? How are you improving the lives of others around you?

9. You serve gratefully, love generously, and give so much of yourself unendingly. What will you do for yourself, to enjoy life? (Example: Taking a trip, spa day, therapeutic massage)

10. List three goal-oriented girlfriends, who can empower you to galvanize your greatness. What qualities do they bring to the table?

a.

b.

c.

11. What you speak into the atmosphere will eventually appear. What personal quotes or excerpts from this book, will you use to speak over your life and into the lives of others?

a.

b.

c.

On a scale from 1 to 10, rate each of the following statements below, as it applies to your thoughts and what you believe. **1** means you strongly disagree. **10** means you strongly agree.

Statement	Rating
1. I have a strong prayer life and relationship with God.	_____
2. I love and value myself.	_____
3. I feel valued in my relationships.	_____
4. My job/career is satisfying and rewarding.	_____
5. I am optimistic about life.	_____
6. I respect myself.	_____
7. I like the direction where my life is going.	_____
8. I have someone in my life, that I can open up to.	_____
9. I like the woman that I see in the mirror.	_____
10. My relationships are positive and they help me to grow daily.	_____
11. I believe that God has greater things, ahead for me and my family.	_____
Total Score	_____

WISDOM FOR A WINNING WOMAN

- Develop a strong relationship with God.

- Focus on your goals and maintain a positive mindset.

- Your health is your wealth.

- Renew your mind, body, and spirit.

- Release and let go of the past.

- Forgive yourself and others.

- Surround yourself with people, who motivate you to be a better you.

- Focus more on what you can give, rather than what you can receive.

- Speak up for yourself and remain determined, to achieve your dream.

- Define your happiness and personal success.

- Pursue your purpose and be a goal-getter.

- Embrace your beauty and find the blessing in every lesson.

- Stir and work your gifts, they will take you from local to global.

- Love yourself, celebrate your growth, know your worth.

ACKNOWLEDGMENTS

Undoubtedly, the idea for *Woman,* was inspired by my previous book *Dear Queen.* As a continuation, I wanted to immerse many of the principles and concepts together, by providing cohesion to the content presented. Since *Dear Queen* is the how, undoubtedly *Woman* is the why, that expresses the essence of one's significance in an intimate and intricate way. I was compelled to write this book, because I believe your why provides direction for your life. How to wear your crown is essential, but why you should wear it reveals your identity and royalty in a unique way.

My sincerest appreciation is extended to my Norbrook Publishing family, for their tireless and tremendous efforts. Thank you to my Mama Dr. Janice Connor, my brother Elijah, Don Smith, and Hawk. I'm grateful for all of the pastors, journalists, and business leaders, who have poured into me and found wisdom from my words. Much love and thanks to you all, especially to every *WOMAN*, who reads this book and wears her crown.

ABOUT THE AUTHOR

Dr. Eddie Connor is a bestselling author, college professor, international speaker, and TV host on TCT Network. He is a survivor of stage four cancer and empowers people to overcome obstacles. Dr. Connor is the cousin, of one of the world's most influential entertainers and musicians, the late legendary Prince.

As an author of eight bestselling books, Dr. Connor has been featured and hosted segments on BET, CBS, FOX, NBC, PBS, The Steve Harvey TV Show, The Tom Joyner Show, and The Word Network. He has been a guest on *The Potter's Touch* and as an empowerment speaker at Bishop T.D. Jakes' *MegaFest*. He was also featured in the acclaimed BET documentary, *It Takes a Village to Raise Detroit*.

He is the founder of the mentoring program, *Boys 2 Books*, which empowers young males via literacy, leadership, and life skills enrichment. The program became the impetus for President Barack Obama's, *My Brother's Keeper* initiative.

Dr. Connor is a recipient of *The President Barack Obama Volunteer Service Award* and *The President Barack Obama Lifetime Achievement Award* from The White House. He is recognized as one of the *Top 35 Millennial Influencers in America*, listed in the *Top 100 Leaders in Who's Who in Black Detroit*, and named to *Michigan Chronicle's Top 40 under 40*.

As a sought after communicator and motivator, he speaks extensively at churches, colleges, and conferences. Dr. Connor grew up in Kingston, Jamaica and lives in Detroit, Michigan. **Visit www.EddieConnor.com**

CONNECT WITH DR. EDDIE CONNOR

To request Dr. Eddie Connor for speaking engagements, media interviews, or for bulk book purchases, please email: **info@EddieConnor.com**

WEBSITE:
www.EddieConnor.com

SOCIAL MEDIA:
Facebook.com/EddieConnorJr
Instagram: @EddieConnorJr
Twitter: @EddieConnorJr
Youtube.com/EddieConnor
#WomanTheBook

Made in the USA
Columbia, SC
09 August 2018